America's Best Cheesecakes

To Linda Larsen!

Joyce Ryan

Joyce Ryan

**BUTTERFLY
BOOKS**

Published by Butterfly Books
4210 Misty Glade
San Antonio, Texas 78247
Telephone 210-494-0077

Manufactured in the United States of America

Library of Congress Cataloging-in-Publication Data

Ryan, Joyce.
    America's best cheesecakes / by Joyce Ryan.
        p.   cm.
    Includes index.
    ISBN 0-939077-06-X
    1. Cheesecake (Cookery)   I. Title.
  TX773.R93 1998
  641.8'653--dc21   97-31656
                                              CIP

ISBN: 0-939077-06-X

Front Cover: Classic Cheesecake (see page 10)
              with Fresh Fruit (see page 12)

Contents

★★★

Introduction

Chapter 1
Success Tips 6

Chapter 2
Classic Cheesecake 10

Chapter 3
Chocolate Cheesecakes 20

Chapter 4
Coffee Cheesecakes 36

Chapter 5
Fruit Cheesecakes 45

Chapter 6
Layered Cheesecakes 62

Chapter 7
Marbled Cheesecakes 74

Chapter 8
Peanut Butter Cheesecakes 82

Chapter 9
Six-Inch Cheesecakes 88

Chapter 10
Special Cheesecakes 93

Chapter 11
Spirited Cheesecakes 107

Index 125

Dedication

To my husband Jim, my sweetheart, and to my little poodle, Beaujolais, my sweetie-pie.

About the Author

Joyce Ryan is an expert cook as well as author and artist. She has written 8 books and had 13 one-woman shows. Listed in Who's Who, her artwork is in private collections throughout the United States, Europe, Japan, and Korea.

Also by Joyce Ryan

Happy Camper's Gourmet Cookbook
Drawing at Home
Calligraphy: Elegant and Easy
Traveling with Your Sketchbook
Seoul Travel Guide
Scenes of Southern Arizona
Seoul Sketches

Acknowledgments

My appreciation and thanks to Corinne Price for her intelligent editorial assistance. Very special thanks to Jim Klar for his helpful criticism and professional advise. And to Mother, the best cook in the world, for teaching me how to cook and instilling in me the desire to excel.

Introduction

★★★

"We're having cheesecake for dessert," is a magical proclamation that sets the stage for an eagerly anticipated event. Blissful memories of cheesecake's superb taste and elegant appearance explain why this spectacular dessert is so popular. Almost everyone craves a slice of this irresistible treat.

Surprisingly enough, this scrumptious dessert is easy to prepare. Success requires no technical expertise and can be ensured by following several simple guidelines. Predictable, reliable results are gained from reading, then following easy-to-understand instructions, not from professional cooking skills.

AMERICA'S BEST CHEESECAKES begins with practical information that takes the mystery out of cheesecake preparation. For your convenience, "Ten Cheesecake Commandments" summarizes the important points of this chapter.

Chapter Two is devoted to the "Classic Cheesecake." The delectable cheesecake from this basic recipe can be varied more than 33 ways. Select from an assortment of toppings, additional ingredients, crusts, and decorations. If you prefer, reduce the size of the cheesecake or prepare a cheesecake pie or tart.

Additional chapters feature a variety of flavors. Choose from chocolate, coffee, spirited, fruit, peanut butter, marbled, layered, and special flavors.

If you cook for only one or two people, try a six-inch cheesecake recipe. Chapter Nine highlights small cheesecake recipes that yield reduced quantity, but not reduced quality. These marvelous little cheesecakes also make much-appreciated gifts.

Baking cheesecake is a fabulous pastime that gives you a tasty reward for your efforts. Try one recipe and you are certain to prepare more. This addictive hobby will make you a truly cherished family member and a celebrity with your friends.

1
Success Tips
★★★

Baking a cheesecake is easy if you follow a few basic guidelines. For your convenience, a summary of this information is listed in my "Ten Cheesecake Commandments" on page 9.

Use a Springform Pan
● Always bake your cheesecake in a springform pan. A springform pan is a two-part pan consisting of a bottom and a detachable side. You release the side of the pan from the bottom with a spring located on the side. The springform pan's clever design enables you to make attractive presentations and slice the cake with ease.
● I recommend you first cover the pan bottom with aluminum foil before attaching it to the side. This facilitates cleanup and enables you to transfer your cake onto a serving platter.
● If you are serving your cheesecake at a friend's house, the pan bottom is likely to get misplaced. You can avoid this possibility by transferring your cake to a 9-inch, round cardboard base. Use the foil to lift the cake off the pan bottom to the cardboard base, then tuck the excess foil underneath the base.
● To avoid possible cake mixture leaks, always place your springform pan on a pizza pan or baking sheet while baking.
● Springform pans come in different sizes. Most of my recipes call for a 9-inch springform pan. If you use a smaller pan, the filling may overflow while baking. If you use a larger pan, reduce the baking time.

How to Mix
● For the creamiest cheesecake, always mix your ingredients with either a hand-held or heavy-duty electric mixer on low speed. It is important when mixing to scrape the sides of the bowl with your spatula.
● For the creamiest results, always bring ingredients to room temperature before mixing. Bring cream cheese to room temperature by cutting the cold cream cheese into cubes, then placing in a large microwave-safe bowl. Microwave for 1 to 2 minutes, stopping and stirring as needed. Or, soften in a warm oven for 10 minutes. To quickly bring eggs to room temperature, submerge in warm water for 5 to 10 minutes.

• The basic mixing procedure is as follows: Beat the cheese with the mixer until it is light and fluffy, adding sugar gradually while scrapping the sides of the bowl with a spatula. Add eggs, one at a time, beating until just blended, then add remaining ingredients. Mix until smooth, being careful not to overmix.

Maximum Flavor
• All my cheesecake recipes, except one, call for cream cheese. I prefer cream cheese because it yields the smoothest, creamiest texture.
• For best results, make your cheesecake one day in advance of serving. The cheesecake needs time for its flavors to mellow.
• Serve thoroughly chilled to further enhance the flavor of the cheesecake.

Doneness Test
• Bake the minimum time suggested, then check. The sides should be slightly puffed and the center set. The center will jiggle like Jell-O when moved. When you press the center with your finger it will spring back. If the center appears wet and shiny, bake the cheesecake several more minutes, then test again.
• Doneness is actually a matter of personal preference. I like a rich, creamy texture. If you prefer a more dense, firm texture, bake the cheesecake longer. The center will not jiggle when moved. Be forewarned, however, if you bake the cheesecake longer, it is much more likely to crack.

Preventing Cracks
• When mixing the cheesecake batter, do not overbeat after adding the eggs.
• Use a 300° oven temperature. Cheesecakes are egg-based, therefore necessitate low heat. Correct temperature is critical. If your cheesecakes crack, your oven temperature reading may be incorrect. Lower the temperature and increase the baking time.
• When baking do not open the door until the cheesecake has reached the minimum cooking time.
• The best way to prevent cracks is to bake the cheesecake in a bain-marie (water bath). Why? The hot water surrounding the cake ensures even heat distribution and compensates for shrinkage as moisture evaporates from the cheesecake during baking. Proceed as follows: Securely cover the outside of your cheesecake pan with heavy-duty foil. This tight seal prevents water from leaking into the batter. Press crust into the pan, then pour in the filling. Place the filled springform pan in a large pan, such as a roaster. Place roaster in oven. Carefully pour boiling water into the roaster so that it comes halfway up the side of your springform pan. I prefer to use a large

measuring cup for adding the water because it keeps me from accidentally pouring water into the batter. Baking time is usually increased when using a bain-marie. Using a bain-marie to bake a cheesecake is not mandatory; however, this method eliminates most cracking problems.

● After removing the pan from the oven, immediately run a hot, wet knife around the inside edge of the pan to loosen the cheesecake. This allows the cheesecake to shrink as it cools without cracking.

● Place the cheesecake on a wire rack and cool at room temperature for 1 hour before refrigerating. Cooling the cheesecake too quickly can cause it to crack.

● In summary, cracks are caused by the following errors: Overbeating the batter after adding the eggs; baking at too high heat; opening the oven door before the cheesecake is almost done; and cooling too quickly.

Healing Cracks

● No matter how many precautions you take, cracks occur occasionally. Do not worry, you are not alone; this also holds true for professional chefs. Simply add a topping or garnish to cover up the crack. For example, a dollop of whipped cream or fresh fruit looks great and tastes delicious.

● If you prefer, chill the cheesecake overnight; then heal the crack by smoothing the surface with a knife that has been dipped in hot water. When healing a chocolate cheesecake, use a hot dry knife.

Cutting the Cheesecake

● Slice the cheesecake with a sharp, hot, wet knife. Hold the knife under a hot faucet or dip in hot water, then slice. Wipe off the knife as often as necesary.

● Cutting the cheesecake with waxed or unwaxed (not minted) dental floss is also effective. Stretching and holding the floss taunt, press through the cake. Pull the floss out from the bottom of the cheesecake. Do not pull the floss up through the cake. Some crusts need to be cut with a sharp knife.

Transferring the Cheesecake

● Remove the side of the pan by releasing the spring, then lift the side of the pan straight up to separate it from the cake. Blot excess moisture on top of the cheesecake with a tissue. A paper towel leaves a texture. Transfer the cake to the serving plate. Add garnishes.

● Be advised, when serving your cake without removing the pan bottom, the metal bottom slides. Be careful not to tip the serving platter when transferring the cheesecake to the table, otherwise the cheesecake will fly off!

Freezing and Thawing Cheesecakes
● Chill an ungarnished cheesecake thoroughly in the refrigerator. Place it in a large freezer bag and seal, then freeze. If you prefer, double bag for extra protection. The cheesecake will keep for several months.
● Thaw in refrigerator overnight or at room temperature for 2 to 3 hours. Add chilled or cooked toppings and garnishes after the cheesecake has thawed.

Food Safety
● Refrigerate leftovers for safe storage. Cover pan with foil, then chill.

Ten Cheesecake Commandments
A Summary of Success Tips

1. **Do** make the cheesecake 24 hours in advance of serving.
2. **Do** bake the cheesecake in a springform pan.
3. **Do** use room-temperature ingredients for the best results.
4. **Do** mix the cheesecake with an electric mixer on low speed.
5. **Do not** overbeat the batter after adding the eggs.
6. **Do** place the cheesecake pan on a pizza pan or baking sheet to prevent possible leaks.
7. **Do not** bake the cheesecake in a higher than 300° oven.
8. **Do not** open the oven door until the cheesecake has reached its minimum cooking time.
9. **Do** run a knife around inside rim of cheesecake after removing from oven.
10. **Do** cool the cheesecake on a wire rack for 1 hour before refrigerating.

2
Classic Cheesecake
★★★

"Classic Cheesecake" is a fabulously delicious and attractive dessert. The cheesecake's rich, creamy flavor and impressive appearance are deceptive though, because the preparation is surprisingly simple. Try the recipe once and you are certain to bake it again. Your friends and family will insist!

If you prefer, vary the recipe by adding an ingredient, topping, or decoration. Changing the crust offers additional possibilities. In fact, this chapter features more than 33 ways to personalize "Classic Cheesecake."

Classic Cheesecake

Crust:
2 cups graham cracker crumbs
1/4 cup sugar
1/4 cup margarine, softened
Filling:
3 8-ounce packages cream cheese, softened
1¼ cups sugar
3 eggs
1 cup sour cream
2 teaspoons vanilla extract

1. In a small bowl stir together crust ingredients. Press firmly onto bottom and halfway up sides of a 9-inch springform pan.
2. In a large bowl using an electric mixer, beat cream cheese until light and fluffy. Gradually beat in sugar. Add eggs, one at a time, beating at low speed until blended. Add sour cream and vanilla, beating at low speed until well combined. Pour mixture into crust.
3. Bake in a preheated 300° oven for 50 to 60 minutes. Cheesecake is done when it springs back when lightly touched in the center (cheesecake will shake slightly when moved). Remove the cake from the oven and run a knife around the inside edge of pan.
4. Cool cheesecake on wire rack at room temperature for 1 hour. Cover pan with foil, then chill overnight. Serves 12 to 18.

Additions

Vary the flavor of "Classic Cheesecake" by adding one or more ingredients. Pour half of the filling into the crust, then sprinkle with half of the ingredient(s) you have selected. Gently spoon remaining filling into pan. Sprinkle evenly with the remaining portion of ingredient(s). Bake, cool, and chill as directed for "Classic Cheesecake." Additional ingredients I suggest include:

- 1 cup semisweet chocolate chips
- 1 cup miniature semisweet chocolate chips
- 1 cup butterscotch chips
- 1 cup milk chocolate chips
- 1 cup peanut butter chips
- 1/3 cup each semisweet chocolate chips, milk chocolate chips, butterscotch chips, and peanut butter chips
- 2 cups chopped Snickers or Baby Ruth candy bars
- 1 3/4 cups of 1/2-inch cubed brownies (Freeze before cutting for best results. Substitute with a Chocolate Cookie Crust, if you prefer. See page 16.)
- 1 cup candied fruit and 1/2 cup chopped nuts
- 3/4 cup canned pie filling (Drop spoonfuls of pie filling over cream cheese filling.)
- 1½ cups coarsely chopped Oreo cookies (Substitute with a Chocolate Cookie Crust, if you prefer. See page 16.)

Toppings

Enhance the flavor of "Classic Cheesecake" with a tasty and elegant topping. Prepare the cheesecake as directed (if preferred, including additions), then follow instructions for the topping of your choice. Choose a topping that compliments the character of your cheesecake's flavor. The topping can also improve the appearance of the cheesecake by covering up unsightly cracks.

BAKED TOPPINGS

Prepare crust and filling as directed for "Classic Cheesecake," then follow directions for the topping of your choice.

Sour Cream Topping

Bake cheesecake until almost done. Remove the cheesecake from the oven. Mix 1 1/3 cups sour cream and 2 tablespoons sugar. Spread topping evenly over cake. Return the cake to a 300° oven for 3 to 5 minutes to set topping. Cool and chill as directed for "Classic Cheesecake."

Spirited Sour Cream Topping
Bake cheesecake until almost done. Remove the cheesecake from the oven. Add 2 tablespoons liqueur to Sour Cream Topping (see page 11). Suggestions include Kahlúa, amaretto, and Curaçao. Prepare as directed for Sour Cream Topping.

Swirl
Pour filling into crust. Pipe or drizzle 1/4 cup fruit preserves or ice cream topping over filling. Cut through mixture with knife to create marble effect. Bake, cool, and chill as directed for "Classic Cheesecake."

Peanut Butter Topping
Bake cheesecake until almost done. Remove cheesecake from the oven. In a small bowl using an electric mixer, beat 3 tablespoons creamy peanut butter with 1/2 cup light brown sugar. Add 1 cup sour cream and 1 teaspoon vanilla extract, beating until well combined. Spread mixture over cheesecake. Return the cake to a 300° oven for 3 to 5 minutes to set topping. Cool and chill as directed for "Classic Cheesecake."

S'Mores Topping
Prepare crust and filling as directed for "Classic Cheesecake." Bake, cool, and chill. Sprinkle 1½ cups miniature marshmallows and 2/3 to 3/4 cup milk chocolate chips over the cheesecake. Broil briefly until marshmallows are toasted and chips are softened. Serve cheesecake immediately.

CHILLED TOPPINGS
Prepare crust and filling as directed for "Classic Cheesecake." Bake, cool and chill, then follow directions for the topping of your choice.

Fruit Pie Filling
Spread desired amount of canned fruit pie filling over chilled cheesecake. Cherry and blueberry are my personal favorites.

Whipped Cream
Frost chilled cheesecake with whipped cream, then sprinkle with cinnamon, cocoa, crushed cookies (Vanilla Wafers, Oreos, Graham Crackers, or Ginger Snaps), ground coffee, or lemon, orange, or lime rind.

Fresh Fruit
Decorate chilled cake with fresh fruit of the season. Use one variety or a combination of fruits.

Ambrosia
2½ cups orange sections cut into bite-size pieces
1/2 cup flaked coconut, packed
1 to 2 tablespoons confectioners' sugar
6 drained maraschino cherries, quartered

Mix together all ingredients. Spoon desired amount of topping over chilled cheesecake. Pass remaining topping.
VARIATION: Substitute cubed pineapple for orange pieces.

Stenciled Topping
Blot cheesecake with tissue to remove excess moisture. Lay a doily or cut-paper stencil on the cheesecake. Sift confectioners' sugar, Cinnamon-Sugar, or Cocoa-Sugar over doily. Carefully remove doily.
Cinnamon-Sugar: Mix together 2 tablespoons sugar and 1½ teaspoons cinnamon.
Cocoa-Sugar: Mix together 2 tablespoons unsweetened cocoa powder and 1 teaspoon sugar.

Sliced Fruit
Thinly slice oranges, lemons, or limes. Arrange on a chilled cheesecake.

COOKED TOPPINGS
Prepare crust and filling for "Classic Cheesecake" as directed. Bake, cool and chill, then follow directions for the topping of your choice.

Cranberry Amaretto Topping
1 16-ounce can whole berry cranberry sauce
1/4 cup sugar
1 tablespoon cornstarch
1/4 cup amaretto
Garnish:
Sliced or slivered almonds

1. In small saucepan over medium heat, bring cranberry sauce and sugar to boil. Reduce to low heat, stirring occasionally, until sugar is dissolved.
2. Mix cornstarch and amaretto until smooth. Add to cranberry mixture. Simmer on low to medium heat, stirring constantly, until sauce is thickened. Cool to room temperature.
3. Stir, then spread desired amount over chilled cheesecake. Chill until topping is set, about 1 hour.
4. Garnish rim of cheesecake with sliced or slivered almonds.

13

Lemon Curd
1/4 cup butter
3/4 cup sugar
1 teaspoon grated lemon rind
3 eggs, beaten
1/4 cup lemon juice
1 drop yellow food coloring
Garnish:
Lemon slice twist (see page 17)
Mint leaf

1. Place butter, sugar, rind, beaten eggs, and lemon juice in the top of a double boiler over simmering water. Cook, stirring constantly until thick, approximately 5 minutes. Do not boil mixture.
2. Remove from heat. Stir in food coloring. Strain mixture into bowl. Cover with plastic wrap, pressing directly onto surface. Chill 2 hours or overnight.
3. Spread mixture over chilled cheesecake. Chill until topping is set, about 1 hour.
4. Garnish with a lemon slice twist and mint leaf in center of cake. Or, cut individual servings and place lemon slice twist and mint leaf on each slice.

Pineapple Topping
1/2 cup sugar
2 tablespoons cornstarch
1 20-ounce can crushed pineapple in juice, undrained
1 tablespoon butter

1. In a small saucepan stir together sugar and cornstarch. Add pineapple and butter. Heat over medium heat until thickened, stirring constantly.
2. Cool to room temperature. Spread over chilled cheesecake. Chill until topping is set, about 1 hour.

Chocolate Glaze
Place 6 ounces semisweet chocolate, 2 tablespoons butter, and 1/4 cup milk in a small microwave-safe bowl. Microwave until melted. Stop and stir until completely smooth. Cool 15 minutes. Remove sides of pan. Spread glaze over top and sides of chilled cake. Chill until topping is set, about 30 minutes.
Best when the crust is only on the bottom and not on the sides of the cheesecake.

Milk Chocolate Glaze
In a double boiler over hot, but not boiling water, place 1 11½-ounce package milk chocolate chips and 1/4 cup milk. Melt, stirring constantly until smooth.

Cool 10 minutes. Remove sides of the pan. Spread glaze over top and sides of chilled cake. Chill until topping is set, about 1 hour. Best when the crust is only on the bottom and not on the sides of the cheesecake.

Vanilla Glaze
In double boiler over hot, but not boiling water, place 1 1/3 cups vanilla-flavored chips and 3 tablespoons milk. Melt, stirring constantly until smooth. Cool 10 minutes. Remove sides of pan. Spread glaze over top and sides of chilled cake. Chill until topping is set, about 1 hour. This glaze does not harden like a chocolate glaze. Best when the crust is only on the bottom and not on the sides of the cheesecake.

Fruit Juice Glaze
1 tablespoon cornstarch
3 tablespoons sugar
1/2 cup frozen juice concentrate, thawed
2 tablespoons water
1/2 teaspoon almond extract, vanilla extract, or imitation
    strawberry extract

1. In a small saucepan stir together cornstarch and sugar. Add juice concentrate and water gradually, stirring until smooth. Cook over medium heat until thickened.
2. Remove from heat and stir in extract. Cool 5 minutes. Spread over chilled cheesecake. Chill until topping is set, about 30 minutes.

Fruit Preserves Topping
Heat 1/3 cup fruit preserves in the microwave to thin. Spread over chilled cheesecake. Chill until topping is set, about 30 minutes.

Ice Cream Topping
Heat a 11 to 12-ounce jar caramel or hot fudge topping until warm. Spread desired amount over chilled cheesecake.

Turtle Topping
Heat 1/2 cup caramel topping until warm. Spread over top of chilled cake. In a double boiler over hot, but not boiling water, place 3/4 cup milk chocolate chips, 1 tablespoon butter, and 4 teaspoons milk. Melt, stirring constantly until smooth. With spoon, drizzle desired amount of chocolate mixture in parallel lines over caramel topping. (If you use all of the chocolate mixture it will completely cover the top of the cheesecake.) Sprinkle with 1/3 cup chopped pecans. Chill until topping is soft-set, about 25 minutes.

Crusts

Most people consider the cheesecake's crust secondary to the melt-in-your-mouth cream cheese filling. Nonetheless, subtle changes in the crust recipe can enrich the flavor of your cheesecake.

Vary the basic Graham Cracker Crust by substituting an equal amount of Vanilla Wafer, Ginger Snap, or chocolate cookie crumbs for the graham cracker crumbs. You can reduce the sugar to suit your taste, starting with 2 tablespoons. For chocolate cookie crumb crust I prefer to use melted margarine instead of softened margarine.

For a nutty flavor and texture, substitute 1/2 cup finely chopped nuts for 1/2 cup graham cracker crumbs. The nuts add taste and crunch. I recommend almonds, pecans, walnuts, and hazelnuts for interesting flavor variations.

Cinnamon and coffee offer subtle complements to many flavors. Add 1 teaspoon cinnamon or 1 teaspoon instant coffee to your favorite crust ingredients.

Decorations

An unadorned cheesecake is simply elegant, but a garnished cheesecake becomes an instant culinary masterpiece. Give your cheesecake a professional bakery appearance by crowning it with one of the following easy-to-make decorations.

CHOCOLATE DRIZZLE
1/4 cup semisweet chocolate chips
1½ teaspoons shortening

1. Place chocolate chips and shortening in a small microwave-safe bowl. Microwave until melted. Stop and stir until completely smooth.
2. Pour mixture into a decorator bag fitted with a round tip. Pipe the design of your choice over the cheesecake. Try a squiggle design, lattice, or diagonal lines.

WHITE CHOCOLATE DRIZZLE
2 ounces white chocolate, coarsely chopped
1½ teaspoons shortening

1. Place white chocolate and shortening in a small microwave-safe bowl. Microwave on defrost setting until melted. Stop and stir until completely smooth.

2. Pour mixture into a decorator bag fitted with a round tip. Pipe the design of your choice over the cheesecake. Try a squiggle design, lattice, or diagonal lines.

CHOCOLATE LEAVES
Nonpoisonous leaves (rose, lemon, geranium, gardenia, grape, magnolia, nasturtium, or violet)
Semisweet chocolate squares, semisweet chocolate chips, milk chocolate bar, milk chocolate chips, white chocolate, or white baking bar

1. Wash leaves and pat dry. Set aside.
2. Melt chocolate. Using a pastry brush or knife tip, coat the underside of the leaf with 1/8-inch thick chocolate. Chocolate should be spread almost to the edge of the leaf, without touching the edge. Avoid getting chocolate on the front side of the leaf. Place coated leaves on a wax paper-lined plate.
3. Refrigerate until firm. Remove from refrigerator and carefully pull off leaf. Store, in a covered bowl, in refrigerator until time to use.
VARIATIONS:
If you prefer, substitute butterscotch chips, peanut butter chips, or vanilla-flavored chips for the chocolate.

CHOCOLATE DIPPED FRUIT
Fruit (strawberries, pineapple cubes, or orange sections)
1 cup milk chocolate chips
2 teaspoons shortening

1. Wash fruit. Set aside.
2. Melt chips and shortening in a double boiler over hot, but not boiling, water. Stir until smooth.
3. Remove pan from heat. Dip fruit into chocolate. Place on wax paper-lined plate. Chill until set.

STRAWBERRY FANS
Wash and dry strawberries. Using a sharp knife, cut fruit into 4 to 6 equal sections by slicing vertically from the stem to the tip of the berry. Do not cut through the stem. Fan the sections apart and garnish cheesecake.

FRUIT SLICE TWISTS
Lemons, limes, or oranges

1. Slice fruit horizontally into circles.
2. Slice circles from the center to the edge with one cut. Twist the sections in opposite directions, then place on dessert.

Smaller Cheesecakes

When you crave cheesecake, but do not need a large dessert, reduce "Classic Cheesecake" by preparing "One-Pound Classic Cheesecake," "Cheesecake Tart," or "Cheesecake Pie." Although these recipes yield fewer servings, the quality of the flavor and texture remains equally superb.

One-Pound Classic Cheesecake

Crust:
2 cups graham cracker crumbs
1/4 cup sugar
1/4 cup margarine, softened
Filling:
2 8-ounce packages cream cheese, softened
3/4 cup sugar
2 eggs
2/3 cup sour cream
1 teaspoon vanilla extract

1. In a small bowl stir together crust ingredients. Press firmly onto bottom and halfway up sides of a 9-inch springform pan.
2. In a large bowl using an electric mixer, beat cream cheese until light and fluffy. Gradually beat in sugar. Add eggs, one at a time, beating at low speed until blended. Add sour cream and vanilla, beating at low speed until well combined. Pour mixture into crust.
3. Bake in a preheated 300° oven for 40 to 50 minutes. Cheesecake is done when it springs back when lightly touched in center. Remove the cake from the oven and run a knife around the inside edge of the pan.
4. Cool cheesecake on wire rack at room temperature for 1 hour. Cover pan with foil, then chill overnight. Serves 10 to 16.

Classic Cheesecake Tart

Crust:
1½ cups graham cracker crumbs
2 tablespoons sugar
5 tablespoons margarine, melted

Filling:
1 8-ounce package cream cheese, softened
7 tablespoons sugar
1 egg
6 tablespoons sour cream
1 teaspoon vanilla extract, scant

1. In a small bowl stir together crust ingredients. Press firmly onto bottom and 1-inch up sides of a 9-inch springform pan.
2. In a medium bowl using an electric mixer, beat cream cheese until light and fluffy. Gradually beat in sugar. Add egg, sour cream, and vanilla. Beat at low speed until well combined. Pour mixture into crust.
3. Bake in a preheated 300° oven for 20 to 25 minutes. Filling is set, but not firm. The filling will stick to your finger if you press the center of the cheesecake.
4. Cool tart on wire rack for 30 minutes. Cover pan with foil, then chill for 4 hours or overnight. If preferred, add a topping. Serves 6 to 8.

Classic Cheesecake Pie

Crust:
1½ cups graham cracker crumbs
2 tablespoons sugar
5 tablespoons margarine, melted
Filling:
1 8-ounce package cream cheese, softened
7 tablespoons sugar
1 egg
6 tablespoons sour cream
1 teaspoon vanilla extract, scant

1. In a small bowl stir together crust ingredients. Press firmly onto bottom and sides of a 9-inch glass pie plate. Do not place crust on the rim; it will burn.
2. In a medium bowl using an electric mixer, beat cream cheese until light and fluffy. Gradually beat in sugar. Add egg, sour cream, and vanilla. Beat at low speed until well combined. Pour mixture into crust. The filling will not completely fill the pan; there will be a 1/2-inch margin.
3. Bake in a preheated 300° oven for 20 to 25 minutes. Filling is set, but not firm. The filling will stick to your finger if you press the center of the cheesecake.
4. Cool pie on wire rack for 30 minutes. Cover pan with foil, then chill for 4 hours or overnight. If preferred, add a topping. Serves 6 to 8.

3
Chocolate Cheesecakes
★★★
Chocolate Almond Cheesecake

Crust:
3/4 cup graham cracker crumbs
1/2 cup ground almonds
3 tablespoons sugar
3 tablespoons margarine, melted
Filling:
3 8-ounce packages cream cheese, softened
1¼ cups sugar
3 eggs
1 cup sour cream
1/3 cup sifted unsweetened cocoa powder
2 teaspoons almond extract, heaping
1 teaspoon vanilla extract
Topping:
2 cups Cool Whip, thawed
1/4 teaspoon almond extract
Garnish:
Sliced almonds

1. In a small bowl stir together crust ingredients. Press firmly onto bottom of a 9-inch springform pan.
2. In a large bowl using an electric mixer, beat cream cheese until light and fluffy. Gradually beat in sugar. Add eggs, one at a time, beating at low speed until blended. Add remaining filling ingredients, beating at low speed until well combined. Pour mixture into crust.
3. Bake in a preheated 300° oven for 50 to 60 minutes. Cheesecake is done when it springs back when lightly touched in the center (cheesecake will shake slightly when moved). Remove the cake from the oven and run a knife around the inside edge of pan.
4. Cool cheesecake on wire rack at room temperature for 1 hour. Cover pan with foil, then chill overnight.
5. In a small bowl stir together topping ingredients. Spread over cheesecake, then sprinkle with sliced almonds. Serves 12 to 18.

Chocolate Brownie Cheesecake

Crust:
1½ cups chocolate cookie crumbs
3 tablespoons margarine, melted
Filling:
3 8-ounce packages cream cheese, softened
1 cup sugar
3 eggs
1 cup sour cream
1 cup semisweet chocolate chips, melted
2 teaspoons vanilla extract
1 3/4 cups of 1/2-inch cubed brownies (Freeze before cutting for best results.)

1. In a small bowl stir together crust ingredients. Press firmly onto bottom of a 9-inch springform pan.
2. In a large bowl using an electric mixer, beat cream cheese until light and fluffy. Gradually beat in sugar. Add eggs, one at a time, beating at low speed until blended. Add sour cream, melted chocolate chips, and vanilla. Beat at low speed until well combined.
3. Pour one-third filling into crust. Sprinkle with one-third brownie cubes. Gently spoon one-third filling into pan, then sprinkle again with one-third brownie cubes. Gently spoon remaining filling into pan and sprinkle with remaining brownie cubes. Press to make the top surface as even as possible.
4. Bake in a preheated 300° oven for 50 to 60 minutes. Cheesecake is done when it springs back when lightly touched in the center (cheesecake will shake slightly when moved). Remove the cake from the oven and run a knife around the inside edge of pan.
5. Cool cheesecake on wire rack at room temperature for 1 hour. Cover pan with foil, then chill overnight. Serves 12 to 18.

Chocolate Coconut Cheesecake

Crust:
1 ¼ cups graham cracker crumbs
2 tablespoons sugar
3 tablespoons margarine, softened
Filling:
3 8-ounce packages cream cheese, softened
1 ¼ cups sugar
3 eggs
1 cup sour cream
1 3½-ounce can flaked coconut
1/3 cup sifted unsweetened cocoa powder
1 tablespoon imitation coconut extract
1 teaspoon vanilla extract
1/2 teaspoon almond extract
Garnish:
Flaked coconut
Coarsely grated chocolate

1. In a small bowl stir together crust ingredients. Press firmly onto bottom of
a 9-inch springform pan.
2. In a large bowl using an electric mixer, beat cream cheese until light and
fluffy. Gradually beat in sugar. Add eggs, one at a time, beating at low speed
until blended. Add remaining filling ingredients, beating at low speed until well
combined. Pour mixture into crust.
3. Bake in a preheated 300° oven for 50 to 60 minutes. Cheesecake is done when
it springs back when lightly touched in center (cheesecake will shake slightly
when moved). Remove the cake from the oven and run a knife around the inside
edge of pan.
4. Cool cheesecake on wire rack at room temperature for 1 hour. Cover pan with
foil, then chill overnight.
5. Garnish with flaked coconut and grated chocolate. Serves 12 to 18.

Chocolate Fudge Cheesecake

Crust:
2 cups chocolate cookie crumbs
1/4 cup margarine, melted
Filling:
3 8-ounce packages cream cheese, softened
2/3 cup sugar
4 eggs
1 14-ounce can sweetened condensed milk
1 12-ounce package semisweet chocolate chips, melted
2 teaspoons vanilla extract

1. In a small bowl stir together crust ingredients. Press firmly onto bottom and halfway up sides of a 9-inch springform pan.
2. In a large bowl using an electric mixer, beat cream cheese until light and fluffy. Gradually beat in sugar. Add eggs, one at a time, beating at low speed until blended. Add remaining ingredients, beating at low speed until well combined. Pour mixture into crust.
3. Bake in a preheated 300° oven for 45 to 55 minutes. Cheesecake is done when it springs back when lightly touched in the center (cheesecake will shake slightly when moved). Remove the cake from the oven and run a knife around the inside edge of pan.
4. Cool cheesecake on wire rack at room temperature for 1 hour. Cover pan with foil, then chill overnight. Serves 12 to 18.

CHOCOLATE FUDGE 'N' CHIP CHEESECAKE
Prepare crust and filling as directed for Chocolate Fudge Cheesecake. Pour half the filling into crust. Sprinkle 1/2 cup chips of your choice over filling. I recommend semisweet chocolate, vanilla-flavored, peanut butter, or miniature semisweet chocolate chips. Gently spoon remaining filling into pan. Sprinkle with an additional 1/2 cup chips. Bake, cool, and chill as directed for Chocolate Fudge Cheesecake.

Chocolate Honey Cheesecake

Crust:
2 cups graham cracker crumbs
1/4 cup sugar
1/4 cup margarine, softened
Filling:
2 8-ounce packages cream cheese, softened
2/3 cup honey
2 eggs
1/2 cup sour cream
1 4-ounce package German sweet chocolate, melted
1 teaspoon vanilla extract

1. In a small bowl stir together crust ingredients. Press firmly onto bottom and halfway up sides of a 9-inch springform pan.
2. In a large bowl using an electric mixer, beat cream cheese until light and fluffy. Beat in honey. Add eggs, one at a time, beating at low speed until blended. Add remaining ingredients, beating at low speed until well combined. Pour mixture into crust.
3. Bake in a preheated 300° oven for 55 to 65 minutes. The cheesecake is done when it shakes slightly when moved. (The batter is very sticky. Unlike other cheesecakes when done, the batter will stick to your finger when pressed in the center.) Remove the cake from the oven and run a knife around the inside edge of the pan.
4. Cool cheesecake on wire rack at room temperature for 1 hour. Cover pan with foil, then chill overnight. Serves 10 to 16.

Chocolate Malted Milk Cheesecake

Crust:
1½ cups chocolate cookie crumbs
3 tablespoons margarine, melted
Filling:
3 8-ounce packages cream cheese, softened
1 cup sugar
3 eggs
1 cup sour cream
1¼ cups Kraft instant chocolate malted milk or Carnation chocolate malted milk
2 teaspoons vanilla extract
1 cup coarsely chopped Whoppers malted milk candy

1. In a small bowl stir together crust ingredients. Press firmly onto bottom of
a 9-inch springform pan.
2. In a large bowl using an electric mixer, beat cream cheese until light and
fluffy. Gradually beat in sugar. Add eggs, one at a time, beating at low
speed until blended. Add sour cream, chocolate malted milk, and vanilla. Beat
at low speed until well combined.
3. Pour half the filling into crust. Sprinkle with 1/2 cup chopped Whoppers.
Gently spoon remaining batter into pan. Sprinkle evenly with remaining candy.
4. Bake in a 300° oven for 1 hour to 1 hour and 10 minutes. Cheesecake is done
when it springs back when lightly touched in the center (cheesecake will shake
slightly when moved). Remove the cake from the oven and run a knife around
the inside edge of pan.
5. Cool cheesecake on wire rack at room temperature for 1 hour. Cover pan
with foil, then chill overnight. Serves 12 to 18.

Chocolate Maple Pecan Cheesecake

Crust:
1 cup graham cracker crumbs
1/4 cup chopped pecans, toasted
2 tablespoons sugar
2 tablespoons margarine, softened
Filling:
3 8-ounce packages cream cheese, softened
1/2 cup sugar
4 eggs
1 14-ounce can sweetened condensed milk
1 cup semisweet chocolate chips, melted
2 teaspoons imitation maple extract
1/2 cup chopped pecans, toasted
Glaze:
3 ounces semisweet chocolate
1 tablespoon butter
Coating:
1/2 to 3/4 cup finely chopped pecans, toasted

1. In a small bowl stir together crust ingredients. Press firmly onto bottom of a 9-inch springform pan.
2. In a large bowl using an electric mixer, beat cream cheese until light and fluffy. Gradually beat in sugar. Add eggs, one at a time, beating at low speed until blended. Add sweetened condensed milk, melted chocolate chips, and maple extract. Beat at low speed until well combined. Pour mixture into crust. Sprinkle with chopped pecans.
3. Bake in a preheated 300° oven for 45 to 55 minutes. Cheesecake is done when it springs back when lightly touched in the center (cheesecake will shake slightly when moved). Remove the cake from the oven and run a knife around the inside edge of pan.
4. Cool cheesecake on wire rack at room temperature for 1 hour. Cover pan with foil, then chill overnight.
5. Place chocolate and butter in a small microwave-safe bowl. Microwave until melted. Stop and stir until completely smooth. Place cheesecake on a rack with a sheet of wax paper underneath. With knife apply glaze to side of cake. Gently pat the finely chopped pecans onto the sides. Chill until coating is set, about 15 minutes. Serves 12 to 18.

CHOCOLATE WALNUT CHEESECAKE
Substitute chopped walnuts for chopped pecans in the crust, filling, and coating. Delete maple extract. Add 2 teaspoons imitation black walnut extract. Follow directions for Chocolate Maple Pecan Cheesecake.

Chocolate Raspberry Cheesecake

Crust:
1½ cups chocolate cookie crumbs
3 tablespoons margarine, melted
Filling:
3 8-ounce packages cream cheese, softened
1 1/3 cups sugar
3 eggs
3/4 cup sour cream
1/2 cup raspberry schnapps
1 cup semisweet chocolate chips, melted
2 teaspoons vanilla extract
Topping:
1 1/3 cups sour cream
1/3 cup sugar
Garnish:
Raspberries

1. In a small bowl stir together crust ingredients. Press firmly onto bottom of a 9-inch springform pan.
2. In a large bowl using an electric mixer, beat cream cheese until light and fluffy. Gradually beat in sugar. Add eggs, one at a time, beating at low speed until blended. Add remaining filling ingredients, beating at low speed until well combined. Pour mixture into crust.
3. Bake in a preheated 300° oven for 50 to 60 minutes. Cheesecake is done when it springs back when lightly touched in the center (cheesecake will shake slightly when moved).
4. Remove the cake from the oven. In a small bowl stir together topping ingredients. Spread evenly over cheesecake. Return the cake to the oven for 3 to 5 minutes or until topping is set. Remove the cake from the oven and run a knife around the inside edge of pan.
5. Cool cheesecake on wire rack at room temperature for 1 hour. Cover pan with foil, then chill overnight.
6. Garnish cake with raspberries. Serves 12 to 18.

★★★★★★★★★★★★★★★★★★★★★★★★

Chocolate Spiderweb Cheesecake

Crust:
2 cups chocolate cookie crumbs
1/4 cup margarine, melted
Basic Filling:
3 8-ounce packages cream cheese, softened
2/3 cup sugar
4 eggs
1 14-ounce can sweetened condensed milk
2 teaspoons vanilla extract
White Chocolate Filling:
1/4 cup basic filling
1 ounce white chocolate, melted
Chocolate Filling:
4 3/4 cups basic filling
1 12-ounce package semisweet chocolate chips, melted
Garnish:
5 to 6 stems of small white silk flowers
1. In a small bowl stir together crust ingredients. Press firmly onto bottom and halfway up sides of a 9-inch springform pan.
2. In a large bowl using an electric mixer, beat cream cheese until light and fluffy. Gradually beat in sugar. Add eggs, one at a time, beating at low speed until blended. Add sweetened condensed milk and vanilla, beating at low speed until well combined.
3. For white chocolate filling transfer 1/4 cup basic filling to a small bowl. To this, stir in melted white chocolate. Set aside. This will be used to create the design on the top of the cake.
4. For chocolate filling add melted chocolate chips to remaining filling. Stir until well combined. Pour mixture into crust.
5. Pour white chocolate filling into a decorator bag fitted with a round tip. Pipe a spiral of 5 to 6 circles, ending in the center. With knife tip, pull 8 to 10 rows across the circles from the center to the outer edge.
6. Bake in a preheated 300° oven for 45 to 55 minutes. Cheesecake is done when it springs back when lightly touched in the center (cheesecake will shake slightly when moved). Remove the cake from the oven and run a knife around the inside edge of pan.
7. Cool cheesecake on wire rack at room temperature for 1 hour. Cover pan with foil, then chill overnight.
8. Place cheesecake on serving platter. Garnish by arranging silk flowers around base of cheesecake. Serves 12 to 18.
FEATHER DESIGN:
Prepare the crust, white chocolate filling, and chocolate filling as directed for Chocolate Spiderweb Cheesecake. Instead of a spiral, pipe 10 to 11 rows, forming a loop when reaching the end of each row. With knife tip, make 10 to 11 rows at a right angle to the piped rows. Bake, cool, and chill as directed for Chocolate Spiderweb Cheesecake.

MARBLE DESIGN:
Prepare the crust and basic filling as directed for Chocolate Spiderweb
Cheesecake. For white chocolate filling stir together melted white chocolate and
1/3 cup basic filling, not 1/4 cup basic filling. For chocolate filling add melted
chocolate chips to remaining filling, stirring until well combined. Pour chocolate
filling into crust. Drop spoonfuls of white chocolate filling over chocolate
filling. Cut through mixtures with knife for marble effect. Bake, cool, and chill
as directed for Chocolate Spiderweb Cheesecake.

Chocolate Truffle Cheesecake

Crust:
2 cups graham cracker crumbs
1/4 cup sugar
1/4 cup margarine, softened
Filling:
16 ounces milk chocolate, chopped
3 8-ounce packages cream cheese, softened
1 cup sugar
4 eggs
1 cup sour cream
1/4 teaspoon salt
2 teaspoons vanilla extract
Garnish:
Whipped cream
Grated milk chocolate

1. In a small bowl stir together crust ingredients. Press firmly onto bottom
and halfway up sides of a 9-inch springform pan.
2. In a double boiler over hot, but not boiling water, melt the milk chocolate.
Stir constantly while melting. Set aside to cool.
3. In a large bowl using an electric mixer, beat cream cheese until light and
fluffy. Gradually beat in sugar. Add eggs, one at a time, beating at low
speed until blended. Add melted milk chocolate, sour cream, salt, and vanilla.
Beat at low speed until blended. Pour mixture into crust.
4. Bake in a preheated 300° oven for 1 hour and 10 minutes to 1 hour
and 20 minutes. Cheesecake is done when it springs back when lightly pressed
in center (cheesecake will shake slightly when moved). Remove the cake from
the oven and run a knife around the inside edge of pan.
5. Cool cheesecake on wire rack at room temperature for 1 hour. Cover pan
with foil, then chill overnight.
6. Garnish cheesecake with large dollop of whipped cream placed in the
center of the cake. Sprinkle grated milk chocolate over whipped cream.
Serves 12 to 18.

Dutch Chocolate Cheesecake

Crust:
2 cups graham cracker crumbs
1 tablespoon unsweetened Dutch process cocoa
1/4 cup sugar
1/4 cup margarine, softened
Filling:
3 8-ounce packages cream cheese, softened
1 1/3 cups sugar
3 eggs
1 cup sour cream
1/4 cup sifted unsweetened Dutch process cocoa
1 teaspoon vanilla extract
Topping:
1½ cups sour cream
1/3 cup sugar
2 teaspoons unsweetened Dutch process cocoa
Garnish:
Unsweetened Dutch process cocoa

1. In a small bowl stir together crust ingredients. Press firmly onto bottom and halfway up sides of a 9-inch springform pan.
2. In a large bowl using an electric mixer, beat cream cheese until light and fluffy. Gradually beat in sugar. Add eggs, one at a time, beating at low speed until blended. Add remaining filling ingredients, beating at low speed until well combined. Pour mixture into crust.
3. Bake in a preheated 300° oven for 55 to 65 minutes. Cheesecake is done when it springs back when lightly touched in the center (cheesecake will shake slightly when moved).
4. Remove the cake from the oven. In a small bowl stir together topping ingredients. Spread evenly over cheesecake. Return the cake to the oven for 3 to 5 minutes or until topping is set. Remove the cake from the oven and run a knife around the inside edge of pan.
5. Cool cheesecake on wire rack at room temperature for 1 hour. Cover pan with foil, then chill overnight.
6. Garnish cheesecake with a sprinkle of cocoa. Serves 12 to 18.

German Chocolate Cheesecake

Crust:
1¼ cups graham cracker crumbs
2 tablespoons sugar
3 tablespoons margarine, softened
Filling:
3 8-ounce packages cream cheese, softened
1¼ cups sugar
3 eggs
1 cup sour cream
1/4 cup sifted unsweetened cocoa powder
1 teaspoon vanilla extract
Topping:
1/2 cup margarine
1/4 cup light brown sugar, packed
2 tablespoons milk
2 tablespoons light corn syrup
1 3½-ounce can flaked coconut
1/2 cup chopped pecans
1 teaspoon vanilla extract

1. In a small bowl stir together crust ingredients. Press firmly onto bottom
of a 9-inch springform pan.
2. In a large bowl using an electric mixer, beat cream cheese until light and
fluffy. Gradually beat in sugar. Add eggs, one at a time, beating at low speed
until blended. Add remaining filling ingredients, beating at low speed until well
combined. Pour mixture into crust.
3. Bake in a preheated 300° oven for 50 to 60 minutes. Cheesecake is done
when it springs back when lightly pressed in center (cheesecake will shake
slightly when moved). Remove the cake from the oven and run a knife around
the inside edge of pan.
4. Cool cheesecake on wire rack at room temperature for 1 hour. Cover pan
with foil, then chill overnight.
5. In a small saucepan melt margarine. Add brown sugar, milk, and corn syrup.
Cook over medium heat, stirring constantly, until thickened. Remove pan from
heat. Stir in coconut, pecans, and vanilla. Cool for 5 minutes. Spread evenly
over cheesecake. Cover pan with foil, then chill until topping is set,
about 2 hours. Serves 12 to 18.

Mexican Chocolate Cheesecake

Crust:
2 cups graham cracker crumbs
1/4 cup sugar
1 teaspoon cinnamon
1/4 cup margarine, softened
Filling:
3 8-ounce packages cream cheese, softened
1/2 cup sugar
3 eggs
2 tablespoons Kahlúa
4 teaspoons instant coffee
1 14-ounce can sweetened condensed milk
1 cup semisweet chocolate chips, melted
1½ teaspoons cinnamon
Garnish:
Strawberries

1. In a small bowl stir together crust ingredients. Press firmly onto bottom and halfway up sides of a 9-inch springform pan.
2. In a large bowl using an electric mixer, beat cream cheese until light and fluffy. Gradually beat in sugar. Add eggs, one at a time, beating at low speed until blended. Stir together Kahlúa and instant coffee. Add coffee mixture, sweetened condensed milk, melted chocolate chips, and cinnamon to cream cheese mixture. Beat at low speed until well combined. Pour mixture into crust.
3. Bake in a preheated 300° oven for 45 to 55 minutes. Cheesecake is done when it springs back when lightly touched in the center (cheesecake will shake slightly when moved). Remove the cake from the oven and run a knife around the inside edge of pan.
4. Cool cheesecake on wire rack at room temperature for 1 hour. Cover pan with foil, the chill overnight.
5. Garnish with strawberries. Serves 12 to 18.

Milk Chocolate Cheesecake

Crust:
2 cups graham cracker crumbs
1/4 cup sugar
1/4 cup margarine, softened
Filling:
2 8-ounce packages cream cheese, softened
1/2 cup sugar
2 eggs
2/3 cup sour cream
1 cup milk chocolate chips, melted
1 teaspoon vanilla extract
Garnish:
8 to 10 milk chocolate dipped strawberries (see page 17)

1. In a small bowl stir together crust ingredients. Press firmly onto bottom and halfway up sides of a 9-inch springform pan.
2. In a large bowl using an electric mixer, beat cream cheese until light and fluffy. Gradually beat in sugar. Add eggs, one at a time, beating at low speed until blended. Add remaining filling ingredients, beating at low speed until well combined. Pour mixture into crust.
3. Bake in a preheated 300° oven for 40 to 50 minutes. Cheesecake is done when it springs back when lightly touched in the center (cheesecake will shake slightly when moved). Remove the cake from the oven and run a knife around the inside edge of pan.
4. Cool cheesecake on wire rack at room temperature for 1 hour. Cover pan with foil, then chill overnight.
5. Garnish with milk chocolate dipped strawberries. Serves 10 to 16.

Sweet Chocolate Cheesecake

Crust:
1½ cups chocolate cookie crumbs
3 tablespoons margarine, melted
Filling:
3 8-ounce packages cream cheese, softened
1 cup sugar
3 eggs
1 cup sour cream
2 4-ounce packages German sweet chocolate, melted
1 teaspoon vanilla extract
Frosting:
6 ounces German sweet chocolate
2 tablespoons butter
1/2 cup sour cream

1. In a small bowl stir together crust ingredients. Press firmly onto bottom of a 9-inch springform pan.
2. In a large bowl using an electric mixer, beat cream cheese until light and fluffy. Gradually beat in sugar. Add eggs, one at a time, beating at low speed until blended. Add remaining filling ingredients, beating at low speed until well combined. Pour mixture into crust.
3. Bake in a preheated 300° oven for 50 to 60 minutes. Cheesecake is done when it springs back when lightly touched in the center (cheesecake will shake slightly when moved). Remove the cake from the oven and run a knife around the inside edge of pan.
4. Cool cheesecake on wire rack at room temperature for 1 hour. Cover pan with foil, then chill overnight.
5. Place chocolate and butter in a small microwave-safe bowl. Microwave until melted. Stop and stir until completely smooth. Stir in sour cream. Remove sides of the pan. Spread frosting over top and sides of cheesecake. Chill until frosting is set, about 45 minutes. Serves 12 to 18.

White Chocolate Cheesecake

Crust:
1 ¼ cups graham cracker crumbs
2 tablespoons sugar
3 tablespoons margarine, softened
Filling:
3 8-ounce packages cream cheese, softened
1/2 cup sugar
3 eggs
1 cup sour cream
12 ounces white chocolate, melted
1 tablespoon vanilla extract
Garnish:
Strawberry fans (see page 17)

1. In a small bowl stir together crust ingredients. Press firmly onto bottom of a 9-inch springform pan.
2. In a large bowl using an electric mixer, beat cream cheese until light and fluffy. Gradually beat in sugar. Add eggs, one at a time, beating at low speed until blended. Add remaining filling ingredients, beating at low speed until well combined. Pour mixture into crust.
3. Bake in a preheated 300° oven for 50 to 60 minutes. Cheesecake is done when it springs back when lightly touched in the center (cheesecake will shake slightly when moved). Remove the cake from the oven and run a knife around the inside edge of pan.
4. Cool cheesecake on wire rack at room temperature for 1 hour. Cover pan with foil, then chill overnight.
5. Garnish individual slices with a strawberry fan. Serves 12 to 18.

4
Coffee Cheesecakes
★★★

Chocolate Cappuccino Cheesecake

Crust:
2 cups chocolate cookie crumbs
1/4 cup margarine, melted
Filling:
3 8-ounce packages cream cheese, softened
1 ¼ cups sugar
3 eggs
1/2 cup sour cream
1 4-ounce package German sweet chocolate, melted
1/2 cup strong coffee, room temperature
2 tablespoons Kahlúa

1. In a small bowl stir together crust ingredients. Press firmly onto bottom and halfway up sides of a 9-inch springform pan.
2. In a large bowl using an electric mixer, beat cream cheese until light and fluffy. Gradually beat in sugar. Add eggs, one at a time, beating at low speed until blended. Add remaining ingredients, beating at low speed until well combined. Pour mixture into crust.
3. Bake in a preheated 300° oven for 50 to 60 minutes. Cheesecake is done when it springs back when lightly touched in center (cheesecake will shake slightly when moved). Remove the cake from the oven and run a knife around the inside edge of pan.
4. Cool cheesecake on wire rack at room temperature for 1 hour. Cover pan with foil, then chill overnight. Serves 12 to 18.

Coffee Cheesecake

Crust:
1½ cups chocolate cookie crumbs
2 tablespoons light brown sugar, packed
3/4 teaspoon instant coffee
1/2 teaspoon cinnamon
3 tablespoons margarine, melted
Filling:
3 8-ounce packages cream cheese, softened
1¼ cups sugar
3 eggs
3 tablespoons Kahlúa
4 to 5 teaspoons instant coffee
1 cup sour cream
2 drops red food coloring
2 drops green food coloring
Topping:
4 ounces Cool Whip, thawed
3/4 teaspoon instant coffee
Garnish:
Cool Whip
Chocolate leaves (see page 17)

1. In a small bowl stir together crust ingredients. Press firmly onto bottom of a 9-inch springform pan.
2. In a large bowl using an electric mixer, beat cream cheese until light and fluffy. Gradually beat in sugar. Add eggs, one at a time, beating at low speed until blended. Stir together Kahlúa and instant coffee. Add coffee mixture, sour cream, and food coloring to cream cheese mixture. Beat at low speed until well combined. Pour mixture into crust.
3. Bake in a preheated 300° oven for 45 to 55 minutes. Cheesecake is done when it springs back when lightly touched in the center (cheesecake will shake slightly when moved). Remove the cake from the oven and run a knife around the inside edge of pan.
4. Cool cheesecake on wire rack at room temperature for 1 hour. Cover pan with foil, then chill overnight.
5. Remove sides of pan. In a small bowl stir together topping ingredients. Spread over top and sides of cheesecake. Garnish center of cheesecake with a dollop of Cool Whip. Stud dollop with several chocolate leaves. Serves 12 to 18.

Café au Lait Cheesecake

Crust:
2 cups chocolate cookie crumbs
1/4 cup margarine, melted
Basic Filling:
3 8-ounce packages cream cheese, softened
1¼ cups sugar
3 eggs
1 cup sour cream
1 teaspoon vanilla extract
Mocha Filling:
2½ cups basic filling
1 tablespoon Kahlúa
1 tablespoon instant coffee
2 tablespoons sifted unsweetened cocoa powder
2 drops red food coloring
2 drops green food coloring
Garnish:
Whipped cream
Unsweetened cocoa powder

1. In a small bowl stir together crust ingredients. Press firmly onto bottom and halfway up sides of a 9-inch springform pan.
2. In a large bowl using an electric mixer, beat cheese until light and fluffy. Gradually beat in sugar. Add eggs, one at a time, beating at low speed until blended. Add sour cream and vanilla, beating at low speed until well combined.
3. For mocha filling transfer 2½ cups basic filling to a medium bowl. Stir together Kahlúa and instant coffee. Add coffee mixture, cocoa, and food coloring to cream cheese mixture. Beat at low speed until well combined. Pour mixture into crust.
4. Gently spoon remaining basic filling over mocha filling.
5. Bake in a preheated 300° oven for 45 to 55 minutes. Cheesecake is done when it springs back when lightly touched in the center (cheesecake will shake slightly when moved). Remove the cake from the oven and run a knife around the inside edge of pan.
6. Cool cheesecake on wire rack at room temperature for 1 hour. Cover pan with foil, then chill overnight.
7. Spread top of cheesecake with whipped cream, then sprinkle with cocoa. Serves 12 to 18.

Coffee Almond Cheesecake

Crust:
1½ cups chocolate cookie crumbs
2 tablespoons light brown sugar, packed
3/4 teaspoon instant coffee
3 tablespoons margarine, melted
Filling:
3 8-ounce packages cream cheese, softened
1¼ cups sugar
3 eggs
3 tablespoons Kahlúa
4 teaspoons instant coffee
1 cup sour cream
3/4 teaspoon almond extract
2 drops red food coloring
2 drops green food coloring
2/3 cup sliced almonds
Garnish:
Whipped cream
Sliced almonds

1. In a small bowl stir together crust ingredients. Press firmly onto bottom of
a 9-inch springform pan.
2. In a large bowl using an electric mixer, beat cream cheese until light and
fluffy. Gradually beat in sugar. Add eggs one at a time, beating at low speed
until blended. Stir together Kahlúa and instant coffee. Add coffee mixture, sour
cream, almond extract, and food coloring to cream cheese mixture. Beat at low
speed until well combined.
3. Pour half the filling into crust. Sprinkle with 1/3 cup sliced almonds. Gently
spoon remaining filling into pan. Sprinkle evenly with remaining sliced almonds.
4. Bake in a preheated 300° oven for 50 to 60 minutes. Cheesecake is done
when it springs back when lightly touched in the center (cheesecake will shake
slightly when moved).
5. Cool cheesecake on wire rack at room temperature for 1 hour. Cover pan
with foil, then chill overnight.
6. Garnish edge of cheesecake with dollops of whipped cream. Sprinkle with
sliced almonds. Serves 12 to 18.

Chocolate Fudge Espresso Cheesecake

Crust:
2 cups chocolate cookie crumbs
1/4 cup margarine, melted
Filling:
3 8-ounce packages cream cheese, softened
2/3 cup sugar
4 eggs
1/4 cup Kahlúa
3 to 4 tablespoons instant coffee
1 14-ounce can sweetened condensed milk
1 12-ounce package semisweet chocolate chips, melted
2 teaspoons vanilla extract
Garnish:
Whipped cream
Grated semisweet chocolate
Chocolate leaves (see page 17)

1. In a small bowl stir together crust ingredients. Press firmly onto bottom and halfway up sides of a 9-inch springform pan.
2. In a large bowl using an electric mixer, beat cream cheese until light and fluffy. Gradually beat in sugar. Add eggs, one at a time, beating at low speed until blended. Stir together Kahlúa and instant coffee. Add coffee mixture, sweetened condensed milk, melted chocolate chips, and vanilla to cream cheese mixture. Beat at low speed until well combined. Pour mixture into crust.
3. Bake in a preheated 300° oven for 45 to 55 minutes. Cheesecake is done when it springs back when lightly touched in the center (cheesecake will shake slightly when moved). Remove the cake from the oven and run a knife around the inside edge of pan.
4. Cool cheesecake on wire rack at room temperature for 1 hour. Cover pan with foil, then chill overnight.
5. Pipe whipped cream around edge of cheesecake. Sprinkle whipped cream with grated chocolate, then stud with chocolate leaves. Serves 12 to 18.

Espresso Cheesecake

Crust:
1½ cups chocolate cookie crumbs
3 tablespoons margarine, melted
Filling:
3 8-ounce packages cream cheese, softened
3/4 cup sugar
3 eggs
3 tablespoons instant coffee
2 teaspoons vanilla extract
1 14-ounce can sweetened condensed milk
Garnish:
Whipped cream
Finely ground coffee

1. In a small bowl stir together crust ingredients. Press firmly onto bottom of a 9-inch springform pan.
2. In a large bowl using an electric mixer, beat cream cheese until light and fluffy. Gradually beat in sugar. Add eggs, one at a time, beating at low speed until blended. Stir together instant coffee and vanilla. Add coffee mixture and sweetened condensed milk to cream cheese mixture. Beat at low speed until well combined. Pour mixture into crust.
3. Bake in a preheated 300° oven for 40 to 50 minutes. Cheesecake is done when it springs back when lightly touched in the center (cheesecake will shake slightly when moved). Remove the cake from the oven and run a knife around the inside edge of pan.
4. Cool cheesecake on wire rack at room temperature for 1 hour. Cover pan with foil, then chill overnight.
5. Slice cheesecake. Garnish each slice with a dollop of whipped cream, then sprinkle with finely ground coffee. Serves 12 to 18.

ESPRESSO CHOCOLATE CHIP CHEESECAKE
Prepare crust and filling as directed for Espresso Cheesecake. Pour half the filling into crust. Mix 1/2 cup miniature semisweet chocolate chips with 1 teaspoon flour. Sprinkle over filling. Gently spoon remaining filling into pan. Sprinkle with an additional 1/2 cup miniature semisweet chocolate chips. Bake, cool, and chill as directed for Espresso Cheesecake. Delete garnish.

Orange Cappuccino Cheesecake

Crust:
1¼ cups graham cracker crumbs
2 tablespoons sugar
1/2 teaspoon cinnamon
3 tablespoons margarine, softened
Filling:
3 8-ounce packages cream cheese, softened
1¼ cups sugar
3 eggs
1/4 cup orange juice
4 teaspoons instant coffee
3/4 cup sour cream
1/2 teaspoon cinnamon
1 teaspoon grated orange rind
1 teaspoon vanilla extract
Garnish:
Orange slice twist (see page 17)
Grated chocolate

1. In a small bowl stir together crust ingredients. Press firmly onto bottom of a 9-inch springform pan.
2. In a large bowl using an electric mixer, beat cream cheese until light and fluffy. Gradually beat in sugar. Add eggs, one at a time, beating at low speed until blended. Stir together orange juice and instant coffee. Add coffee mixture, sour cream, cinnamon, orange rind, and vanilla to the cream cheese mixture. Beat at low speed until well combined. Pour mixture into crust.
3. Bake in a preheated 300° oven for 55 minutes to 65 minutes. Cheesecake is done when it springs back when lightly touched in the center (cheesecake will shake slightly when moved). Remove the cake from the oven and run a knife around the inside edge of the pan.
4. Cool cheesecake on a wire rack at room temperature for 1 hour. Cover pan with foil, then chill overnight.
5. Garnish with orange slice twist placed in the center of the cheesecake. Sprinkle with grated chocolate. Serves 12 to 18.

Tiramisù Cheesecake

Crust:
1½ cups graham cracker crumbs
2 tablespoons sugar
3 tablespoons margarine, softened
Filling:
3 8-ounce packages cream cheese, softened
1¼ cups sugar
3 eggs
1 tablespoon Kahlúa
4 teaspoons instant coffee
1 cup sour cream
22 to 24 ladyfingers, approximately 3-inches long
1/4 cup dark rum
Garnish:
Whipped cream
Grated semisweet chocolate
26 to 28 ladyfingers, approximately 3-inches long
1½ yards dark red ribbon

1. In a small bowl stir together crust ingredients. Press firmly onto bottom of
a 9-inch springform pan.
2. In a large bowl using an electric mixer, beat cream cheese until light and
fluffy. Gradually beat in sugar. Add eggs, one at a time, beating at low speed
until blended. Stir together Kahlúa and instant coffee. Add coffee mixture
and sour cream to cream cheese mixture. Beat at low speed until well combined.
3. Pour half the filling into crust. Place a layer of ladyfingers, cut side up,
over filling to cover. Drizzle with dark rum. Gently spoon remaining filling into
pan. Some of the ladyfingers may float to the surface.
4. Bake in a preheated 300° oven for 45 to 55 minutes. Cheesecake is done when
it springs back when lightly touched in the center (cheesecake will shake slightly
when moved). Remove the cake from the oven and run a knife around the inside
edge of the pan.
5. Cool cheesecake on wire rack at room temperature for 1 hour. Cover pan with
foil, then chill overnight.
6. Remove sides of pan. Spread whipped cream over top and sides of cheesecake.
Sprinkle grated chocolate on top of cake. Press ladyfingers, with cut side against
cake, around the side. Tie a ribbon around the cake. Serves 12 to 18.

Viennese Coffee Cheesecake

Crust:
2 cups graham cracker crumbs
1/4 cup sugar
1 teaspoon cinnamon
1/4 teaspoon allspice
1/4 cup margarine, softened
Filling:
3 8-ounce packages cream cheese, softened
2/3 cup sugar, heaping
3 eggs
1/4 cup Kahlúa
2 tablespoons instant coffee
1 14-ounce can sweetened condensed milk
1½ teaspoons cinnamon
1/2 teaspoon allspice
1/4 teaspoon nutmeg
2 teaspoons vanilla extract
Garnish:
1/2 cup heavy cream
2 tablespoons sugar
1/4 teaspoon cinnamon
1/8 teaspoon allspice
Dash nutmeg
Cinnamon sticks, broken in half

1. In a small bowl stir together crust ingredients. Press firmly onto bottom and halfway up sides of a 9-inch springform pan.
2. In a large bowl using an electric mixer, beat cream cheese until light and fluffy. Gradually beat in sugar. Add eggs, one at a time, beating at low speed until blended. Stir together Kahlúa and instant coffee. Add coffee mixture, sweetened condensed milk, spices, and vanilla to cream cheese mixture. Beat at low speed until well combined. Pour mixture into crust.
3. Bake in a preheated 300° oven for 40 to 50 minutes. Cheesecake is done when it springs back when lightly touched in the center (cheesecake will shake slightly when moved). Remove the cake from the oven and run a knife around the inside edge of pan.
4. Cool cheesecake on wire rack at room temperature for 1 hour. Cover pan with foil, then chill overnight.
5. Whip cream until stiff peaks form. Gradually beat in sugar and spices. Place dollops of whipped cream around edge of cheesecake. Stud each dollop with a cinnamon stick. Serves 12 to 18.

5
Fruit Cheesecakes
★★★

Apple Pie Cheesecake

Crust:
2 cups graham cracker crumbs
1/4 cup sugar
1 teaspoon cinnamon
1/4 cup margarine, softened
Filling:
3 8-ounce packages cream cheese, softened
1¼ cups sugar
4 eggs
1/3 cup sour cream
1/2 cup frozen apple juice concentrate, thawed
1 tablespoon lemon juice
1½ teaspoons cinnamon
1/2 teaspoon nutmeg
20-ounce can sliced apples, drained
Garnish:
10 to 12 reserved canned sliced apples

1. In a small bowl stir together crust ingredients. Press firmly onto bottom and
halfway up sides of a 9-inch springform pan.
2. In a large bowl using an electric mixer, beat cream cheese until light and
fluffy. Gradually beat in sugar. Add eggs, one at a time, beating at low speed
until blended. Add sour cream, apple juice concentrate, lemon juice, and spices.
Beat at low speed until well combined.
3. Reserve 10 to 12 sliced apples for garnish, then place remaining sliced apples
into crust. Gently spoon filling into pan over sliced apples. Arrange reserved
sliced apples on top of the cheesecake like the spokes of a wheel.
4. Bake in a preheated 300° oven for 1 hour and 30 minutes to 1 hour
and 40 minutes. Cheesecake is done when it springs back when lightly touched
in the center (cheesecake will shake slightly when moved). Remove the cake
from the oven and run a knife around the inside edge of the pan.
5. Cool cheesecake on wire rack at room temperature for 1 hour. Cover pan
with foil, then chill overnight. Serves 12 to 18.

Apricot Cheesecake

Crust:
3/4 cup graham cracker crumbs
1/2 cup ground almonds
3 tablespoons sugar
1 teaspoon finely grated orange rind
3 tablespoons margarine, melted
Filling:
3 8-ounce packages cream cheese, softened
1¼ cups sugar
4 eggs
3/4 cup sour cream
1/4 cup apricot-flavored brandy
1/2 teaspoon almond extract
1 teaspoon vanilla extract
1 cup chopped canned apricots, drained
Topping:
1½ cups sour cream
3 tablespoons sugar
1 tablespoon apricot brandy
Apricot Roses:
15 to 20 dried apricot halves
Light corn syrup

1. In a small bowl stir together crust ingredients. Press firmly onto bottom of a 9-inch springform pan.
2. In a large bowl using an electric mixer, beat cream cheese until light and fluffy. Gradually beat in sugar. Add eggs, one at a time, beating at low speed until blended. Add sour cream, brandy, and extracts. Beat at low speed until well combined.
3. Pour half the filling into crust. Sprinkle with 1/2 cup chopped apricots. Gently spoon remaining filling into pan. Sprinkle with remaining chopped apricots.
4. Bake in a preheated 300° oven for 1 hour to 1 hour and 10 minutes. Cheesecake is done when it springs back when lightly touched in the center (cheesecake will shake slightly when moved).
5. Remove the cake from the oven. In a small bowl stir together topping ingredients. Spread evenly over cheesecake. Return the cake to the oven for 3 to 5 minutes or until topping is set. Remove the cake from the oven and run a knife around the inside edge of pan.

6. Cool cheesecake on wire rack at room temperature for 1 hour. Cover pan with foil, then chill overnight.

7. Garnish with apricot roses. Place dried apricot halves between two sheets of wax paper. With rolling pin, firmly roll until each apricot half is almost double in size. For each rose, roll up one apricot half very tightly for the center, then loosely wrap 3 or 4 more apricot halves around the center, pinching together at the bottom. For a glossy finish, brush rose with light corn syrup. Prepare additional roses, then arrange on the cake. Serves 12 to 18.

Banana Cheesecake

Crust:
1½ cups chocolate cookie crumbs
3 tablespoons margarine, melted
Filling:
3 8-ounce packages cream cheese, softened
1 cup sugar
3 eggs
1/2 cup sour cream
2/3 cup puréed banana
2/3 cup banana schnapps
2 teaspoons vanilla extract
5 drops yellow food coloring
Garnish:
Banana
Grated semisweet chocolate

1. In a small bowl stir together crust ingredients. Press firmly onto bottom of a 9-inch springform pan.

2. In a large bowl using an electric mixer, beat cream cheese until light and fluffy. Gradually beat in sugar. Add eggs, one at a time, beating at low speed until blended. Add remaining filling ingredients, beating at low speed until well combined. Pour mixture into crust.

3. Bake in a preheated 300° oven for 1 hour to 1 hour and 10 minutes. Cheesecake is done when it springs back when lightly touched in the center (cheesecake will shake slightly when moved). Remove the cake from the oven and run a knife around the inside edge of pan.

4. Cool cheesecake on wire rack at room temperature for 1 hour. Cover pan with foil, then chill overnight.

5. Peel a banana, then roll in grated chocolate; slice. Arrange banana slices on cake. Serves 12 to 18.

Berry Cheesecake

Crust:
2 cups graham cracker crumbs
1/4 cup sugar
1 teaspoon cinnamon
1/4 cup margarine, softened
Filling:
3 8-ounce packages cream cheese, softened
1 ¼ cups sugar
3 eggs
1 cup sour cream
2 tablespoons apricot-flavored brandy
1 teaspoon imitation strawberry extract
1 teaspoon vanilla extract
1 teaspoon almond extract
1/2 cup frozen blueberries, unthawed
1/2 cup frozen red raspberries, unthawed
1/2 cup chopped strawberries
Garnish:
5 strawberries
Red raspberries
Blueberries

1. In a small bowl stir together crust ingredients. Press firmly onto bottom and halfway up sides of a 9-inch springform pan.
2. In a large bowl using an electric mixer, beat cream cheese until light and fluffy. Gradually beat in sugar. Add eggs, one at a time, beating at low speed until blended. Add sour cream, brandy, and extracts. Beat at low speed until well combined.
3. Pour one-third filling into crust. Sprinkle with one-third berries. Gently spoon one-third filling into pan, then sprinkle again with one-third berries. Gently spoon remaining filling into pan and sprinkle with remaining berries.
4. Bake in a preheated 300° oven for 1 hour to 1 hour and 10 minutes. Cheesecake is done when it springs back when lightly touched in center (cheesecake will shake slightly when moved). Remove the cake from the oven and run a knife around the inside edge of pan.
5. Cool cheesecake on wire rack at room temperature for 1 hour. Cover pan with foil, then chill overnight.

6. Place strawberries in center of cake forming a star pattern (stems toward center). Sprinkle red raspberries and blueberries around the strawberries. Serves 12 to 18.

Coconut Cheesecake

Crust:
2 cups graham cracker crumbs
1/4 cup sugar
1/4 cup margarine, softened
Filling:
3 8-ounce packages cream cheese, softened
1 cup sugar
3 eggs
1/2 cup sour cream
1/2 cup cream of coconut
1 3½-ounce can flaked coconut
1/2 teaspoon almond extract
1 teaspoon vanilla extract
Garnish:
Whipped cream
Flaked coconut

1. In a small bowl stir together crust ingredients. Press firmly onto bottom and halfway up sides of a 9-inch springform pan.
2. In a large bowl using an electric mixer, beat cream cheese until light and fluffy. Gradually beat in sugar. Add eggs, one at a time, beating at low speed until blended. Add remaining filling ingredients, beating at low speed until well combined. Pour mixture into crust.
3. Bake in a preheated 300° oven for 55 to 65 minutes. Cheesecake is done when it springs back when lightly touched in the center (cheesecake will shake slightly when moved). Remove the cake from the oven and run a knife around the inside edge of pan.
4. Cool cheesecake on wire rack at room temperature for 1 hour. Cover pan with foil, then chill overnight.
5. Spread top of cheesecake with whipped cream, then sprinkle with flaked coconut. Serves 12 to 18.

Cranberry Vanilla Cheesecake

Crust:
1¼ cups graham cracker crumbs
2 tablespoons sugar
3 tablespoons margarine, softened
Filling:
3 8-ounce packages cream cheese, softened
1 cup sugar
3 eggs
1 cup sour cream
1 6-ounce package white baking bar, melted
1 tablespoon vanilla extract
1 cup sweetened dried cranberries
Garnish:
Whipped cream
Sweetened dried cranberries

1. In a small bowl stir together crust ingredients. Press firmly onto bottom of a 9-inch springform pan.
2. In a large bowl using an electric mixer, beat cream cheese until light and fluffy. Gradually beat in sugar. Add eggs, one at a time, beating at low speed until blended. Add sour cream, melted white baking bar, and vanilla. Beat at low speed until well combined.
3. Pour half the filling into crust. Sprinkle with 1/2 cup dried cranberries. Gently spoon remaining filling into pan. Sprinkle evenly with remaining dried cranberries.
4. Bake in a preheated 300° oven for 50 to 60 minutes. Cheesecake is done when it springs back when lightly touched in the center (cheesecake will shake slightly when moved). Remove the cake from the oven and run a knife around the inside edge of the pan.
5. Cool cheesecake on wire rack at room temperature for 1 hour. Cover pan with foil, then chill overnight.
6. Garnish with whipped cream piped around edge of cheesecake. Sprinkle dried cranberries over the whipped cream. Serves 12 to 18.

Fourth of July Cheesecake

Crust:
1¼ cups graham cracker crumbs
2 tablespoons sugar
3 tablespoons margarine, softened
Filling:
3 8-ounce packages cream cheese, softened
1¼ cups sugar
3 eggs
1 cup sour cream
2 teaspoons vanilla extract
Blueberry Pie Layer:
1¼ cups blueberry pie filling
Garnish:
1/2 to 1 pint blueberries
1½ to 2 pints strawberries

1. In a small bowl stir together crust ingredients. Press firmly onto bottom of a 10-inch springform pan.
2. In a large bowl using an electric mixer, beat cream cheese until light and fluffy. Gradually beat in sugar. Add eggs, one at a time, beating at low speed until blended. Add sour cream and vanilla, beating at low speed until well combined.
3. Spread pie filling over crust. Gently spoon cream cheese mixture over pie filling.
4. Bake in a preheated 300° oven for 1 hour and 10 minutes to 1 hour and 20 minutes. Bake until edges are lightly browned and center is fairly firm. Remove the cake from the oven and run a knife around the inside edge of pan.
5. Cool cheesecake on wire rack at room temperature for 1 hour. Cover pan with foil, then chill overnight.
6. Garnish with a flag design made of fruit. Cover the top left quarter of the cake with blueberries. Hull strawberries, then slice in half vertically. With points facing right, create 3 rows (like stripes) of overlapping strawberries for the quarter of the cake adjacent to the blueberries, and 2 rows in the remaining bottom half of the cake. Serves 12 to 18.

Lemon Cheesecake

Crust:
2 cups graham cracker crumbs
1/4 cup sugar
1/4 cup margarine, softened
Filling:
3 8-ounce packages cream cheese, softened
1 ¼ cups sugar
3 eggs
1/3 cup sour cream
1/2 cup frozen lemonade concentrate, thawed
2 tablespoons lemon juice
1 tablespoon grated lemon rind
1/2 teaspoon almond extract
1 teaspoon vanilla extract
13 drops yellow food coloring
Topping:
1 1/3 cups sour cream
2 tablespoons sugar
4 teaspoons lemon juice
Garnish:
Whipped cream
6 to 8 lemon slice twists (see page 17)

1. In a small bowl stir together crust ingredients. Press firmly onto bottom and halfway up sides of a 9-inch springform pan.
2. In a large bowl using an electric mixer, beat cream cheese until light and fluffy. Gradually beat in sugar. Add eggs, one at a time, beating at low speed until blended. Add remaining filling ingredients, beating at low speed until well combined. Pour mixture into crust.
3. Bake in a preheated 300° oven for 45 to 55 minutes. The cheesecake is done when it springs back when lightly touched in the center (cheesecake will shake slightly when moved).
4. Remove the cake from the oven. In a small bowl stir together topping ingredients. Spread over cheesecake. Return the cake to the oven for 3 to 5 minutes or until topping is set. Remove the cake from the oven and run a knife around the inside edge of pan.
5. Cool cheesecake on wire rack at room temperature for 1 hour. Cover pan with foil, then chill overnight.
6. Garnish with dollops of whipped cream placed around edge of cake. Stud each dollop with a lemon slice twist. Serves 12 to 18.

PINK LEMONADE BIRTHDAY CHEESECAKE
Prepare crust and filling as directed for Lemon Cheesecake, except delete the yellow food coloring. Add 4 drops red food coloring. Bake (including topping), cool, and chill as directed for Lemon Cheesecake. Delete lemon slice twists. Garnish with dollops of whipped cream, birthday candles, and colored sprinkles.

Orange Cheesecake

Crust:
1½ cups chocolate cookie crumbs
3 tablespoons margarine, melted
Filling:
2 8-ounce packages cream cheese, softened
1 1/8 cups sugar
2 eggs
1/2 cup sour cream
1/4 cup frozen orange juice concentrate, unthawed
1 tablespoon grated orange rind
1 teaspoon vanilla extract
5 drops yellow food coloring
5 drops red food coloring
Garnish:
Whipped cream
Chocolate syrup

1. In a small bowl stir together crust ingredients. Press firmly onto bottom of a 9-inch springform pan.
2. In a large bowl using an electric mixer, beat cream cheese until light and fluffy. Gradually beat in sugar. Add eggs, one at a time, beating at low speed until blended. Add remaining filling ingredients, beating at low speed until well combined. Pour mixture into crust.
3. Bake in a preheated 300° oven for 45 to 55 minutes. Cheesecake is done when it springs back when lightly touched in the center (cheesecake will shake slightly when moved). Remove the cake from the oven and run a knife around the inside edge of pan.
4. Cool cheesecake on wire rack at room temperature for 1 hour. Cover pan with foil, then chill overnight.
5. Garnish with dollops of whipped cream around the edge of the cheesecake. Drizzle chocolate syrup over whipped cream. Serves 10 to 16.

Lemon Fudge Vanilla Chip Cheesecake

Crust:
1 ¼ cups graham cracker crumbs
2 tablespoons sugar
3 tablespoons margarine, softened
Filling:
3 8-ounce packages cream cheese, softened
3 eggs
1 14-ounce can sweetened condensed milk
1/2 cup lemon juice
1 tablespoon grated lemon rind, packed
1 teaspoon vanilla extract
1/2 teaspoon almond extract
20 to 25 drops yellow food coloring
1 cup vanilla-flavored chips
1 teaspoon flour
Garnish:
White chocolate leaves (see page 17)

1. In a small bowl stir together crust ingredients. Press firmly onto bottom of
a 9-inch springform pan.
2. In a large bowl using an electric mixer, beat cream cheese until light and
fluffy. Add eggs, one at a time, beating at low speed until blended. Add
sweetened condensed milk, lemon juice, lemon rind, extracts, and food coloring.
Beat at low speed until well combined.
3. Pour half the filling into crust. Mix 1/2 cup vanilla-flavored chips
with 1 teaspoon flour. Sprinkle over filling. Gently spoon remaining filling
into pan. Sprinkle evenly with remaining vanilla-flavored chips.
4. Bake in a preheated 300° oven for 40 to 50 minutes. Cheesecake is done when
it springs back when lightly touched in the center (cheesecake will shake slightly
when moved). Remove the cake from the oven and run a knife around the inside
edge of pan.
5. Cool cheesecake on wire rack at room temperature for 1 hour. Cover pan with
foil, then chill overnight.
6. Garnish with white chocolate leaves. Serves 12 to 18.

Lime Cheesecake

Crust:
2 cups graham cracker crumbs
1/4 cup sugar
1/4 cup margarine, softened
Filling:
3 8-ounce packages cream cheese, softened
1¼ cups sugar
3 eggs
1/3 cup sour cream
1/2 cup frozen limeade concentrate, thawed
2 tablespoons lime juice
1 tablespoon grated lime rind
1/2 teaspoon almond extract
1 teaspoon vanilla extract
3 drops green food coloring
Topping:
1 1/3 cups sour cream
2 tablespoons sugar
4 teaspoons lime juice
Garnish:
Lime slices

1. In a small bowl stir together crust ingredients. Press firmly onto bottom and halfway up sides of a 9-inch springform pan.
2. In a large bowl using an electric mixer, beat cream cheese until light and fluffy. Gradually beat in sugar. Add eggs, one at a time, beating at low speed until blended. Add remaining filling ingredients, beating at low speed until well combined. Pour mixture into crust.
3. Bake in a preheated 300° oven for 40 to 50 minutes. Cheesecake is done when it shakes slightly when moved. (The batter is very sticky. Unlike other cheesecakes when done, the batter will stick to your finger when pressed in the center.)
4. Remove the cake from the oven. In a small bowl stir together topping ingredients. Spread over cheesecake. Return the cake to the oven for 3 to 5 minutes or until topping is set. Remove the cake from the oven and run a knife around the inside edge of pan.
5. Cool cheesecake on wire rack at room temperature for 1 hour. Cover pan with plastic wrap, not foil, then chill overnight.
6. Place overlapping lime slices around edge of cheesecake. Serves 12 to 18.

Peach Melba Cheesecake

Crust:
2 cups graham cracker crumbs
1/4 cup sugar
1/4 cup margarine, softened
Filling:
3 8-ounce packages cream cheese, softened
1¼ cups sugar
3 eggs
3/4 cup sour cream
1/2 cup peach-flavored brandy
1 teaspoon vanilla extract
1 teaspoon almond extract
1 cup chopped fresh peaches
Glaze:
1/3 cup raspberry preserves, heaping
1/4 teaspoon almond extract
Garnish:
Fresh peach slices

1. In a small bowl stir together crust ingredients. Press firmly onto bottom and halfway up sides of a 9-inch springform pan.
2. In a large bowl using an electric mixer, beat cream cheese until light and fluffy. Gradually beat in sugar. Add eggs, one at a time, beating at low speed until blended. Add sour cream, brandy, and extracts. Beat at low speed until well combined.
3. Pour half the filling into crust. Sprinkle with 1/2 cup chopped peaches. Gently spoon remaining filling into pan. Sprinkle with remaining chopped peaches.
4. Bake in a preheated 300° oven for 50 to 60 minutes. Cheesecake is done when it springs back when lightly touched in the center (cheesecake will shake slightly when moved). Remove the cake from the oven and run a knife around the inside edge of pan.
5. Cool cheesecake on wire rack at room temperature for 1 hour. Cover pan with foil, then chill overnight.
6. Heat preserves in microwave to thin. Stir in almond extract. Spread over chilled cheesecake. Chill until topping is set, about 30 minutes.
7. Garnish cheesecake with peach slices, then serve immediately. Serves 12 to 18.

Pineapple Cheesecake

Crust:
2 cups graham cracker crumbs
1/4 cup sugar
1/4 cup margarine, softened
Filling:
3 8-ounce packages cream cheese, softened
1 ¼ cups sugar
3 eggs
1/2 cup sour cream
1 8 ¼-ounce can crushed pineapple in syrup, drained
1/2 cup frozen pineapple juice concentrate, unthawed
1 teaspoon vanilla extract
Garnish:
Whipped cream
Pineapple slices

1. In a small bowl stir together crust ingredients. Press firmly onto bottom and halfway up sides of a 9-inch springform pan.
2. In a large bowl using an electric mixer, beat cream cheese until light and fluffy. Gradually beat in sugar. Add eggs, one at a time, beating at low speed until blended. Add remaining filling ingredients, beating at low speed until well combined. Pour mixture into crust.
3. Bake in a preheated 300° oven for 50 to 60 minutes. Cheesecake is done when it springs back when lightly touched in center (cheesecake will shake slightly when moved). Remove the cake from the oven and run a knife around the inside edge of pan.
4. Cool cheesecake on wire rack at room temperature for 1 hour. Cover pan with foil, then chill overnight.
5. Place whipped cream in a decorator bag fitted with large star tip. Pipe rosettes evenly over entire top of cheesecake. Cut pineapple slices into small wedges. Place point of wedge into rosettes around edge of the cheesecake.
Serves 12 to 18.

Raspberry Cordial Cheesecake

Crust:
1 ¼ cups graham cracker crumbs
2 tablespoons sugar
3 tablespoons margarine, softened
Filling:
3 8-ounce packages cream cheese, softened
4 eggs
1 14-ounce can sweetened condensed milk
1 cup red raspberry preserves
2 tablespoons raspberry schnapps
1 teaspoon almond extract
6 drops red food coloring
Glaze:
1/3 cup semisweet chocolate chips, heaping
1/3 cup milk chocolate chips, heaping
2 tablespoons milk
Garnish:
Chocolate sprinkles

1. In a small bowl stir together crust ingredients. Press firmly onto bottom of
a 9-inch springform pan.
2. In a large bowl using an electric mixer, beat cream cheese until light and
fluffy. Add eggs, one at a time, beating at low speed until blended. Add
remaining filling ingredients, beating at low speed until well combined. The
raspberry preserves remain lumpy. Pour mixture into crust.
3. Bake in a preheated 300° oven for 1 hour and 5 minutes to 1 hour
and 15 minutes. Cheesecake is done when it springs back when lightly touched
in the center (cheesecake will shake slightly when moved). Remove the cake
from the oven and run a knife around the inside edge of pan.
4. Cool cheesecake on wire rack at room temperature for 1 hour. Cover pan
with foil, the chill overnight.
5. Place chips and milk in a small microwave-safe bowl. Microwave until
melted. Stop and stir until mixture is completely smooth. Cool 10 minutes.
Remove sides of pan. Spread glaze over top of cheesecake; do not let topping
run over the side. Scatter chocolate sprinkles evenly over topping. Chill until
the topping is set, about 30 minutes. Serves 12 to 18.

Strawberries 'n' Cream Cheesecake

Crust:
1 ¼ cups graham cracker crumbs
2 tablespoons sugar
3 tablespoons margarine, softened
Filling:
3 8-ounce packages cream cheese, softened
1 ¼ cups sugar
3 eggs
1 cup sour cream
1 tablespoon imitation strawberry extract
1 teaspoon almond extract
5 drops red food coloring
1 cup chopped strawberries
Garnish:
Whipped cream
Strawberries

1. In a small bowl stir together crust ingredients. Press firmly onto bottom of a 9-inch springform pan.
2. In a large bowl using an electric mixer, beat cream cheese until light and fluffy. Gradually beat in sugar. Add eggs, one at a time, beating at low speed until blended. Add sour cream, extracts, and food coloring. Beat at low speed until well combined. With wooden spoon, stir in chopped strawberries. Pour mixture into crust.
3. Bake in a preheated 300° oven for 50 to 60 minutes. Cheesecake is done when it springs back when lightly touched in the center (cheesecake will shake slightly when moved). Remove the cake from the oven and run a knife around the inside edge of pan.
4. Cool cheesecake on wire rack at room temperature for 1 hour. Cover pan with foil, then chill overnight.
5. Spread top of cheesecake with whipped cream, then arrange strawberries around edge. Serves 12 to 18.

Strawberry Cordial Cheesecake

Crust:
1½ cups chocolate cookie crumbs
3 tablespoons margarine, melted
Filling:
3 8-ounce packages cream cheese, softened
4 eggs
1 14-ounce can sweetened condensed milk
1 cup strawberry preserves
1 teaspoon almond extract
1 tablespoon imitation strawberry extract
7 drops red food coloring
Glaze:
6 ounces semisweet chocolate
2 tablespoons butter
1/4 cup milk
Garnish:
Whipped cream
8 to 10 strawberries

1. In a small bowl stir together crust ingredients. Press firmly onto bottom of
a 9-inch springform pan.
2. In a large bowl using an electric mixer, beat cream cheese until light and
fluffy. Add eggs, one at a time, beating at low speed until blended. Add remaining
filling ingredients, beating at low speed until well combined. The preserves will
remain lumpy. Pour mixture into crust.
3. Bake in a preheated 300° oven for 50 to 60 minutes. Cheesecake is done when
it springs back when lightly touched in the center (cheesecake will shake slightly
when moved). Remove the cake from the oven and run a knife around the inside
edge of pan.
4. Cool cheesecake on wire rack at room temperature for 1 hour. Cover pan with
foil, then chill overnight.
5. Place semisweet chocolate, butter, and milk in medium microwave-safe bowl.
Microwave until melted. Stop and stir until completely smooth. Cool 15 minutes.
Remove sides of pan. Spread glaze over top and sides of cheesecake. Chill until
glaze is set, about 30 minutes.
6. Garnish with whipped cream piped around edge of cheesecake. Arrange
strawberries in the whipped cream at regular intervals. Serves 12 to 18.

★★★★★★★★★★★★★★★★★★★★★★★★★★

Sweet Cherry Cheesecake

Crust:
1½ cups chocolate cookie crumbs
3 tablespoons margarine, melted
Filling:
3 8-ounce packages cream cheese, softened
1¼ cups sugar
3 eggs
1/2 cup sour cream
1/3 cup Cherry Herring liqueur
3 tablespoons amaretto
1 teaspoon vanilla extract
1 teaspoon almond extract
2 drops red food coloring
1 cup canned sweet bing cherries, drained
Topping:
1 1/3 cups sour cream
2 tablespoons sugar
1 tablespoon Cherry Herring liqueur
1 tablespoon amaretto
Garnish:
1/2 cup canned sweet bing cherries, drained and patted dry

1. In a small bowl stir together crust ingredients. Press firmly onto bottom of a 9-inch springform pan.
2. In a large bowl using an electric mixer, beat cream cheese until light and fluffy. Gradually beat in sugar. Add eggs, one at a time, beating at low speed until blended. Add sour cream, Cherry Herring liqueur, amaretto, extracts, and food coloring. Beat at low speed until well combined.
3. Pour half the filling into crust. Sprinkle with 1/2 cup sweet cherries. Gently spoon remaining filling into pan. Sprinkle evenly with remaining sweet cherries.
4. Bake in a preheated 300° oven for 1 hour to 1 hour and 10 minutes. The cheesecake is done when it shakes slightly when moved. (The batter is very sticky. Unlike other cheesecakes when done, the batter will stick to your finger when pressed in the center.)
5. Remove the cake from the oven. In a small bowl stir together topping ingredients. Spread evenly over cheesecake. Return the cake to the oven for 3 to 5 minutes or until topping is set. Remove the cake from the oven and run a knife around the inside edge of the pan.
6. Cool cheesecake on wire rack at room temperature for 1 hour. Cover pan with foil, then chill overnight.
7. Garnish edge of cheesecake with sweet cherries. Serves 12 to 18.

61

6
Layered Cheesecakes
★★★

Almond Chocolate Cheesecake

Crust:
1½ cups chocolate cookie crumbs
3 tablespoons margarine, melted
Basic Filling:
3 8-ounce packages cream cheese, softened
4 eggs
1 14-ounce can sweetened condensed milk
2 teaspoons almond extract
1 teaspoon vanilla extract
Chocolate Filling:
3 cups basic filling
1/2 cup semisweet chocolate chips, melted
3 tablespoons sugar
Almond Filling:
2 cups basic filling
1/2 cup sliced almonds
Garnish:
2 to 3 tablespoons sliced almonds

1. In a small bowl stir together crust ingredients. Press firmly onto bottom of a 9-inch springform pan.
2. In a large bowl using an electric mixer, beat cream cheese until light and fluffy. Add eggs, one at a time, beating at low speed until blended. Add sweetened condensed milk and extracts, beating at low speed until well combined.
3. For chocolate filling transfer 3 cups basic filling to a medium bowl. Stir in melted chocolate chips and sugar. Pour chocolate filling into crust.
4. For almond filling add sliced almonds to remaining basic filling. Stir until combined. This batter is very thin. Gently spoon almond filling over chocolate filling.
5. Bake in preheated 300° oven for 40 to 50 minutes. Cheesecake is done when it springs back when lightly touched in the center (cheesecake will shake slightly when moved). Remove the cake from the oven and run a knife around the inside edge of pan.

6. Cool cheesecake on wire rack at room temperature for 1 hour. Cover pan with foil, then chill overnight.
7. Garnish with a sprinkle of sliced almonds. Serves 12 to 18.

Chocolate Vanilla Cheesecake

Crust:
1½ cups chocolate cookie crumbs
3 tablespoons margarine, melted
Basic Filling:
3 8-ounce packages cream cheese, softened
4 eggs
1 14-ounce can sweetened condensed milk
2 teaspoons vanilla extract
Chocolate Filling:
2 cups basic filling
1 cup semisweet chocolate chips, melted
1/3 cup sugar
Vanilla Filling:
3 cups basic filling
2 teaspoons flour
Garnish:
Vanilla leaves (see page 17)
Chocolate leaves (see page 17)

1. In a small bowl stir together crust ingredients. Press firmly onto bottom of an 8-inch springform pan. (A 9-inch springform pan can be substituted, but the thickness of the layers diminishes.)
2. In a large bowl using an electric mixer, beat cheese until light and fluffy. Add eggs, one at a time, beating at low speed until blended. Add sweetened condensed milk and vanilla, beating at low speed until well combined.
3. For chocolate filling transfer 2 cups basic filling to a medium bowl. Stir in melted chocolate chips and sugar until well combined. Pour chocolate filling into crust.
4. For vanilla filling add flour to remaining basic filling. Stir until well combined. Gently spoon vanilla filling over chocolate filling.
5. Bake in a preheated 300° oven for 45 to 55 minutes. Cheesecake is done when it springs back when lightly touched in the center (cheesecake will shake slightly when moved). Remove the cake from the oven and run a knife around the inside edge of pan.
6. Cool cheesecake on wire rack at room temperature for 1 hour. Cover pan with foil, then chill overnight.
7. Garnish with vanilla and chocolate leaves. Serves 12 to 18.

63

★★★★★★★★★★★★★★★★★★★★★★★★

Checkerboard Cheesecake

Equipment:
3 8-inch cake pans
1 plastic ring divider
Crust:
3 cups chocolate cookie crumbs
6 tablespoons margarine, melted
Basic Filling:
3 8-ounce packages cream cheese, softened
4 eggs
1 14-ounce can sweetened condensed milk
1 teaspoon vanilla extract
Chocolate Filling:
2½ cups basic filling
1 cup semisweet chocolate chips, melted
1/3 cup sugar
Butterscotch Filling:
2½ cups basic filling
1 cup butterscotch chips, melted
Chocolate Glaze:
6 ounces semisweet chocolate
2 tablespoons butter

1. Line 3 8-inch cake pans with foil. In a small bowl stir together crust ingredients. Divide mixture evenly among the 3 pans. Press firmly onto bottom of each pan.
2. In a large bowl using an electric mixer, beat cream cheese until light and fluffy. Add eggs, one at a time, beating at low speed until blended. Add sweetened condensed milk and vanilla, beating at low speed until well combined.
3. For chocolate filling transfer 2½ cups basic filling to a medium bowl. To this, stir in melted chocolate chips and sugar.
4. For butterscotch filling add melted butterscotch chips to remaining basic filling. Stir until well combined.
5. Place plastic ring divider into a cake pan. Firmly press divider into crust to avoid leaking. Spoon chocolate filling into outer and inner rings. Spoon butterscotch filling into middle ring. Slowly remove divider and place in another pan. Repeat process for second layer. Slowly remove divider. Wash divider. For third layer firmly press divider into crust. Spoon chocolate filling into middle ring and butterscotch filling into outer and inner rings. Slowly remove divider.
6. Bake in a preheated 300° oven until set and firm, about 25 to 35 minutes.
7. Cool pans on a wire rack for 30 minutes. Cover pans with foil, then chill overnight.

★★★★★★★★★★★★★★★★★★★★★★★★

8. Remove the layers from the pans by carefully peeling off the foil. With crust side down, place a layer with 2 chocolate rings on an 8-inch springform pan bottom. With crust side down, add a layer with 2 butterscotch rings. With crust side down, top with remaining layer with 2 chocolate rings.
9. Place chocolate and butter in a medium microwave-safe bowl. Microwave until melted. Stop and stir until completely smooth. Cool for 15 minutes. Spread glaze over top and sides of cheesecake. Cover, then chill until glaze is set, about 20 minutes. Serves 12 to 18.

Three-Layer Cheesecake

Crust:
2 cups chocolate cookie crumbs
1/4 cup margarine, melted
Filling:
3 8-ounce packages cream cheese, softened
3 eggs
1 14-ounce can sweetened condensed milk
2 teaspoons vanilla extract
Glaze:
1 ¼ cups semisweet chocolate chips
1 ¼ cups milk chocolate chips
6 to 7 tablespoons milk
Garnish:
8 to 12 strawberries

1. Line 3 8-inch cake pans with foil. In a small bowl stir together crust ingredients. Divide mixture evenly among the 3 pans. Press firmly onto bottom of each pan.
2. In a large bowl using an electric mixer, beat cream cheese until light and fluffy. Add eggs, one at a time, beating at low speed until blended. Add sweetened condensed milk and vanilla, beating at low speed until well combined. Divide mixture evenly among the 3 pans.
3. Bake in a preheated 300° oven until set and firm, about 25 to 35 minutes.
4. Cool pans on wire rack at room temperature for 30 minutes. Cover pans with foil, then chill overnight.
5. Place chips and milk in a medium microwave-proof bowl. Microwave until melted. Stop and stir until smooth. Cool 15 minutes.
6. Remove the layers from the pans by carefully peeling off the foil. With crust side down, place a layer on an 8-inch springform pan bottom. Spread with glaze. With crust side down, add the second layer. Spread with glaze. With crust side down, top with remaining layer. Spread glaze over top and sides of cake. Chill until glaze is set, about 20 minutes.
7. Garnish with strawberries. Serves 12 to 18.

65

★★★★★★★★★★★★★★★★★★★★★★

Triple Chocolate Cheesecake

Crust:
3/4 cup chocolate cookie crumbs
1½ tablespoons margarine, melted
Basic Filling:
3 8-ounce packages cream cheese, softened
4 eggs
1 14-ounce can sweetened condensed milk
1 tablespoon vanilla extract
Dark Chocolate Filling:
1½ cups basic filling
1 cup semisweet chocolate chips, melted
3 tablespoons sugar
White Chocolate Filling:
1½ cups basic filling
6 ounces white chocolate, melted
Milk Chocolate Filling:
2 cups basic filling
1/2 cup milk chocolate chips, melted
Garnish:
4 ounces semisweet chocolate
1/2 cup heavy cream

1. Spray the sides of an 8½-inch springform pan with cooking spray. In a small bowl stir together crust ingredients. Press firmly onto bottom of pan. (A 9-inch springform pan can be substituted, but the thickness of the layers diminishes.)
2. In a large bowl using an electric mixer, beat cream cheese until light and fluffy. Add eggs, one at a time, beating at low speed until blended. Add sweetened condensed milk and vanilla, beating at low speed until well combined.
3. For dark chocolate filling transfer 1½ cups basic filling to a medium bowl. To this, stir in melted chocolate chips and sugar. Pour mixture into crust.
4. For white chocolate filling transfer 1½ cups basic filling to a medium bowl. To this, stir in melted white chocolate. Gently spoon over dark chocolate filling.
5. For milk chocolate filling add melted milk chocolate chips to remaining basic filling. Stir until well combined. Gently spoon over white chocolate filling.
6. Bake in a preheated 300° oven for 50 to 60 minutes. Cheesecake is done when it springs back when lightly touched in the center (cheesecake will shake slightly when moved). Remove the cake from the oven and run a knife around the inside edge of pan.
7. Cool cheesecake on wire rack at room temperature for 1 hour. Cover pan with foil, then chill overnight.
8. Place chocolate and cream in a small microwave-safe bowl. Microwave until melted. Stop and stir until completely smooth. Cool 10 minutes. Remove sides

66

of pan. Spread glaze over top and sides of cheesecake. Chill until glaze is set, about 20 minutes. Serves 12 to 18.

Double Chocolate Cheesecake

Crust:
2 cups chocolate cookie crumbs
1/4 cup margarine, melted
Basic Filling:
3 8-ounce packages cream cheese, softened
4 eggs
1 14-ounce can sweetened condensed milk
2 teaspoons vanilla extract
Chocolate Filling:
2½ cups basic filling
1 cup semisweet chocolate chips, melted
1/4 cup sugar
White Chocolate Filling:
2½ cups basic filling
8 ounces white chocolate, melted
Garnish:
Chocolate Drizzle (see page 16)
White Chocolate Drizzle (see page 16)

1. In a small bowl stir together crust ingredients. Press firmly onto bottom and halfway up sides of a 9-inch springform pan.
2. In a large bowl using an electric mixer, beat cream cheese until light and fluffy. Add eggs, one at a time, beating a low speed until blended. Add sweetened condensed milk and vanilla, beating at low speed until well combined.
3. For chocolate filling transfer 2½ cups basic filling to a medium bowl. Stir in melted chocolate chips and sugar until well combined. Pour chocolate filling into crust.
4. For white chocolate filling add melted white chocolate to remaining basic filling. Stir until well combined. Gently spoon white chocolate filling over chocolate filling.
5. Bake in a preheated 300° oven for 50 to 60 minutes. Cheesecake is done when it springs back when lightly touched in the center (cheesecake will shake slightly when moved). Remove the cake from the oven and run a knife around the inside edge of the pan.
6. Cool cheesecake on wire rack at room temperature for 1 hour. Cover pan with foil, then chill overnight.
7. Prepare Chocolate Drizzle. Pour mixture into a decorator bag fitted with a small round tip. Pipe parallel lines across the cake. Prepare White Chocolate Drizzle. Pour mixture into a decorator bag fitted with a small round tip. Pipe parallel lines at right angle to the chocolate lines. Serves 12 to 18.

Valentine Cheesecake

Crust:
2 cups chocolate cookie crumbs
1/4 cup margarine, melted
Filling:
3 8-ounce packages cream cheese, softened
1/4 cup sugar
3 eggs
1 14-ounce can sweetened condensed milk
2 4-ounce packages German sweet chocolate, melted
1 teaspoon vanilla extract
Glaze and Sauce:
1 12-ounce package unsweetened frozen strawberries, thawed
1/2 cup sugar
1 tablespoon cornstarch
1/4 cup water
1 teaspoon almond extract
1 teaspoon vanilla extract
Frosting:
1 4-ounce package German sweet chocolate
2 tablespoons butter
Garnish:
8 to 10 strawberries

1. Line 2 9-inch heart-shaped cake pans with foil. In a small bowl stir together crust ingredients. Divide mixture evenly between the 2 pans. Press firmly onto bottom of each pan.
2. In a large bowl using an electric mixer, beat cream cheese until light and fluffy. Gradually beat in sugar. Add eggs, one at a time, beating at low speed until blended. Add remaining filling ingredients, beating at low speed until well combined. Divide mixture evenly between the 2 pans.
3. Bake in preheated 300° oven until firm, about 25 to 35 minutes.
4. Cool pans on wire rack at room temperature for 30 minutes. Cover each pan with foil, then chill overnight.
5. Remove the layers from the pans by carefully peeling off the foil. With crust side down, place a layer on a foil-covered 9-inch cardboard heart. With crust side down, top with second layer.
6. Purée strawberries in food processor. In medium saucepan mix sugar and cornstarch. Gradually stir in water, then add puréed strawberries. Bring to boil, then reduce heat to simmer. Simmer until mixture thickens, about 3 to 5 minutes. Remove from heat and stir in extracts. Cool mixture to room temperature, then spread about 1/2 to 3/4 cup over top of cheesecake. Leftover glaze will be served as a sauce. Chill cheesecake and sauce while preparing frosting.

★★★★★★★★★★★★★★★★★★★★★★★

7. Place German sweet chocolate and butter in a small microwave-safe bowl. Microwave until melted. Stop and stir until smooth. Using knife, spread frosting on side of cheesecake. Chill until frosting is set, about 20 minutes.
8. Garnish cake with strawberries around top edge. Pass sauce. Serves 12 to 18.

Neapolitan Cheesecake

Crust:
1 cup graham cracker crumbs
2 tablespoons margarine, melted
Basic Filling:
3 8-ounce packages cream cheese, softened
4 eggs
1 14-ounce can sweetened condensed milk
2 teaspoons vanilla extract
Chocolate Filling:
1½ cups basic filling
4 ounces semisweet chocolate, melted
1/4 cup sugar
Strawberry Filling:
1½ cups basic filling
1/3 cup strawberry preserves
1/2 teaspoon almond extract
1/2 teaspoon imitation strawberry extract
3 drops red food coloring
Garnish:
8 to 10 strawberries

1. Spray the sides of an 8-inch springform pan with cooking spray. In a small bowl stir together crust ingredients. Press firmly onto bottom of pan. (A 9-inch springform pan can be substituted, but the thickness of the layers diminishes.)
2. In a large bowl using an electric mixer, beat cream cheese until light and fluffy. Add eggs, one at a time, beating at low speed until blended. Add sweetened condensed milk and vanilla, beating at low speed until well combined.
3. For chocolate filling transfer 1½ cups basic filling to a medium bowl. To this, stir in melted chocolate and sugar. Pour mixture into crust.
4. For strawberry filling transfer 1½ cups basic filling to a a medium bowl. To this, stir in strawberry preserves, extracts, and food coloring. Gently spoon strawberry filling over chocolate filling.
5. Gently spoon remaining basic filling over strawberry filling.
6. Bake in a preheated 300° oven for 45 to 55 minutes. Cheesecake is done when it springs back when lightly touched in the center (cheesecake will shake slightly when moved). Remove the cake from the oven and run a knife around the inside edge of pan.
7. Cool cheesecake on wire rack at room temperature for 1 hour. Cover pan with foil, then chill overnight.
8. Garnish with strawberries. Serves 12 to 18.

Peanut Butter and Jelly Cheesecake

Crust:
1 ¼ cups graham cracker crumbs
2 tablespoons sugar
3 tablespoons margarine, softened
Basic Filling:
3 8-ounce packages cream cheese, softened
3 eggs
1 14-ounce can sweetened condensed milk
2 teaspoons vanilla extract
Peanut Butter Filling:
2 3/4 cups basic filling
9 tablespoons creamy peanut butter
Jelly Filling:
2 cups basic filling
1/2 cup strawberry preserves
1 tablespoon flour
1/2 teaspoon almond extract
1½ teaspoons imitation strawberry extract
3 to 4 drops red food coloring
Garnish:
Strawberries

1. In a small bowl stir together crust ingredients. Press firmly onto bottom of a 9-inch springform pan.
2. In a large bowl using an electric mixer, beat cream cheese until light and fluffy. Add eggs, one at a time, beating at low speed until blended. Add sweetened condensed milk and vanilla, beating at low speed until well combined.
3. For peanut butter filling transfer 2 3/4 cups basic filling to a medium bowl. To this, add peanut butter. Using an electric mixer, beat until well combined. Pour mixture into crust.
4. For jelly filling add preserves, flour, extracts, and food coloring to remaining basic filling. Stir until well combined. Gently spoon strawberry filling over peanut butter filling.
5. Bake in a preheated 300° oven for 50 to 60 minutes. Cheesecake is done when it springs back when lightly touched in the center (cheesecake will shake slightly when moved). Remove the cake from the oven and run a knife around the inside edge of pan.
6. Cool cheesecake on wire rack at room temperature for 1 hour. Cover pan with foil, then chill overnight.
7. Garnish edge of cheesecake with strawberries. Serves 12 to 18.

Triple Delight Cheesecake

Crust:
1½ cups chocolate cookie crumbs
3 tablespoons margarine, melted
Basic Filling:
3 8-ounce packages cream cheese, softened
4 eggs
1 14-ounce can sweetened condensed milk
1 tablespoon vanilla extract
Chocolate Filling:
1½ cups basic filling
3/4 cup semisweet chocolate chips, melted
2 tablespoons sugar
Butterscotch Filling:
1½ cups basic filling
3/4 cup butterscotch chips, melted
Rum Filling:
2 cups basic filling
3/4 teaspoon imitation rum extract
Garnish:
Heath candy bar, chopped

1. Spray the sides of an 8½-inch springform pan with cooking spray. In a small bowl stir together crust ingredients. Press firmly onto bottom of pan. (A 9-inch springform pan can be substituted, but the thickness of the layers diminishes.)
2. In a large bowl using an electric mixer, beat cream cheese until light and fluffy. Add eggs, one at a time, beating at low speed until blended. Add sweetened condensed milk and vanilla, beating at low speed until well combined.
3. For chocolate filling transfer 1½ cups basic filling to a medium bowl. To this, stir in melted chocolate chips and sugar. Pour mixture into crust.
4. For butterscotch filling transfer 1½ cups basic filling to a medium bowl. To this, stir in melted butterscotch chips. Gently spoon over chocolate filling.
5. For rum filling add rum extract to remaining basic filling. Stir until well combined. Gently spoon over butterscotch filling.
6. Bake in a preheated 300° oven for 55 to 65 minutes. Cheesecake is done when it springs back when lightly pressed in center (cheesecake will shake slightly when moved). Remove the cake from the oven and run a knife around the inside edge of pan.
7. Cool cheesecake on wire rack at room temperature for 1 hour. Cover pan with foil, then chill overnight.
8. Garnish cake with chopped candy. Serves 12 to 18.

★★★★★★★★★★★★★★★★★★★★★★★★

Rum Chocolate Cherry Cheesecake

Crust:
1½ cups graham cracker crumbs
2 tablespoons sugar
3 tablespoons margarine, softened
Basic Filling:
3 8-ounce packages cream cheese, softened
4 eggs
1 14-ounce can sweetened condensed milk
1 tablespoon vanilla extract
Chocolate Filling:
2¼ cups basic filling
1 cup semisweet chocolate chips, melted
1/3 cup sugar
1/2 teaspoon cinnamon
Rum Filling:
2 3/4 cups basic filling
2 cups vanilla-flavored chips, melted
1 teaspoon imitation rum extract
Topping:
1 21-ounce can cherry pie filling, chilled
1/8 teaspoon cinnamon

1. In a small bowl stir together crust ingredients. Press firmly onto bottom of a 9-inch springform pan.
2. In a large bowl using an electric mixer, beat cream cheese until light and fluffy. Add eggs, one at a time, beating at low speed until blended. Add sweetened condensed milk and vanilla, beating at low speed until well combined.
3. For chocolate filling remove 2¼ cups basic filling to a medium bowl. To this, stir in melted chocolate chips, sugar, and cinnamon.
4. For rum filling add melted vanilla-flavored chips and rum extract to remaining basic filling. Stir until well combined.
5. Pour rum filling into crust. Gently spoon chocolate filling over rum filling.
6. Bake in a preheated 300° oven for 50 to 60 minutes. Cheesecake is done when it springs back when lightly touched in the center (cheesecake will shake slightly when moved). Remove the cake from the oven and run a knife around the inside edge of pan.
7. Cool cheesecake on wire rack at room temperature for 1 hour. Cover pan with foil, then chill overnight.
8. In a small bowl stir together pie filling and cinnamon. Spread evenly over cheesecake. Serves 12 to 18.

★★★★★★★★★★★★★★★★★★★★★★★

Strawberry Chocolate Cheesecake

Crust:
2 cups chocolate cookie crumbs
1/4 cup margarine, melted
Basic Filling:
3 8-ounce packages cream cheese, softened
4 eggs
1 14-ounce can sweetened condensed milk
2 teaspoons vanilla extract
Chocolate Filling:
2½ cups basic filling
1 cup semisweet chocolate chips, melted
1/3 cup sugar
Strawberry Filling:
2½ cups basic filling
1/2 cup strawberry preserves
1/2 teaspoon almond extract
1½ teaspoons imitation strawberry extract
5 to 6 drops red food coloring
Garnish:
Chocolate Drizzle (see page 16)
8 strawberries

1. In a small bowl stir together crust ingredients. Press firmly onto bottom and halfway up sides of a 9-inch springform pan.
2. In a large bowl using an electric mixer, beat cream cheese until light and fluffy. Add eggs, one at a time, beating at low speed until blended. Add sweetened condensed milk and vanilla, beating at low speed until well combined.
3. For chocolate filling transfer 2½ cups basic filling to a medium bowl. To this, stir in melted chocolate chips and sugar. Pour mixture into crust.
4. For strawberry filling add strawberry preserves, extracts, and food coloring to remaining basic filling. Stir until well combined. Gently spoon strawberry filling over chocolate filling.
5. Bake in a preheated 300° oven for 50 to 60 minutes. Cheesecake is done when it springs back when lightly pressed in center (cheesecake will shake slightly when moved). Remove the cake from the oven and run a knife around the inside edge of pan.
6. Cool cheesecake on wire rack at room temperature for 1 hour. Cover pan with foil, then chill overnight.
7. Prepare Chocolate Drizzle. Using a spoon, drizzle a squiggle design over cheesecake. Chill until drizzle is set, about 10 minutes. Place strawberries around edge of cake. Serves 12 to 18.

7
Marbled Cheesecakes
★ ★ ★

Marbled Cheesecake

Crust:
2 cups chocolate cookie crumbs
1/4 cup margarine, melted
Basic Filling:
3 8-ounce packages cream cheese, softened
1¼ cups sugar
3 eggs
1 cup sour cream
2 teaspoons vanilla extract
Chocolate Filling:
1½ cups basic filling
3 ounces semisweet chocolate, melted
2 tablespoons sugar

1. In a small bowl stir together crust ingredients. Press firmly onto bottom and halfway up sides of a 9-inch springform pan.
2. In a large bowl using an electric mixer, beat cream cheese until light and fluffy. Gradually beat in sugar. Add eggs, one at a time, beating at low speed until blended. Add sour cream and vanilla, beating at low speed until well combined.
3. For chocolate filling transfer 1½ cups basic filling to a small bowl. To this, stir in melted chocolate and sugar. Remove 1/2 cup chocolate filling and reserve. This will be used to create the marble design on the top of the cheesecake.
4. Pour half the basic filling into crust. Drop large spoonfuls of chocolate filling over the basic filling. Gently spoon remaining basic filling into pan. Drop spoonfuls of reserved chocolate filling into pan. Cut through mixtures with knife for marble effect.
5. Bake in a preheated 300° oven for 50 to 60 minutes. Cheesecake is done when it springs back when lightly touched in the center (cheesecake will shake slightly when moved). Remove the cake from the oven and run a knife around the inside edge of pan.
6. Cool cheesecake on wire rack at room temperature for 1 hour. Cover pan with foil, then chill overnight. Serves 12 to 18.

Cheesecake Sundae

Crust:
2 cups chocolate cookie crumbs
1/4 cup margarine, melted
Filling:
3 8-ounce packages cream cheese, softened
1 cup sugar
3 eggs
3/4 cup sour cream
2 teaspoons vanilla extract
1/2 cup Smucker's Hot Fudge Topping
Garnish:
Whipped cream
6 to 8 stemmed maraschino cherries, drained
Smucker's Hot Fudge Topping
Chopped pecans or walnuts
Serve with:
Smucker's Hot Fudge Topping

1. In a small bowl stir together crust ingredients. Press firmly onto bottom and halfway up sides of a 9-inch springform pan.
2. In a large bowl using an electric mixer, beat cream cheese until light and fluffy. Gradually beat in sugar. Add eggs, one at a time, beating at low speed until blended. Add sour cream and vanilla, beating at low speed until well combined.
3. Pour half the filling into crust. Pour 1/4 cup hot fudge topping into a decorator bag fitted with a large round tip. Pipe 5 parallel rows of topping across filling. The topping is very thick; the rows look like ropes. With knife tip, make 5 rows at a right angle to the piped rows. Gently spoon remaining filling into pan. Using remaining 1/4 cup topping, pipe 5 parallel rows across filling. Repeat procedure with knife tip.
4. Bake in a preheated 300° oven for 50 to 60 minutes. Cheesecake is done when it springs back when lightly touched in center (cheesecake will shake slightly when moved). Remove the cake from the oven and run a knife around the inside edge of pan.
5. Cool cheesecake on wire rack at room temperature for 1 hour. Cover pan with foil, then chill overnight.
6. Garnish with 6 to 8 dollops of whipped cream around edge of cheesecake. Place maraschino cherry in center of each dollop. Heat topping. Drizzle topping over whipped cream and cherries, then sprinkle with chopped nuts. Pass additional hot fudge topping. Serves 12 to 18.

★★★★★★★★★★★★★★★★★★★★★★★★★

Chocolate Peanut Butter Marbled Cheesecake

Crust:
1½ cups chocolate cookie crumbs
3 tablespoons margarine, melted
Basic Filling:
3 8-ounce packages cream cheese, softened
4 eggs
1 14-ounce can sweetened condensed milk
1 teaspoon vanilla extract
Chocolate Filling:
3¼ cups basic filling
1/3 cup sugar
1 cup semisweet chocolate chips, melted
Peanut Butter Filling:
1 3/4 cups basic filling
1/2 cup creamy peanut butter

1. In a small bowl stir together crust ingredients. Press firmly onto bottom of a 9-inch springform pan.
2. In a large bowl using an electric mixer, beat cream cheese until light and fluffy. Add eggs, one at a time, beating at low speed until blended. Add sweetened condensed milk and vanilla, beating at low speed until well combined.
3. For chocolate filling transfer 3¼ cups basic filling to a medium bowl. To this, stir in sugar and melted chocolate chips.
4. For peanut butter filling add peanut butter to remaining basic filling. Using an electric mixer, beat at low speed until mixture is smooth. Remove 3/4 cup peanut butter filling and reserve. This will be used to create the marble design on the top of the cheesecake.
5. Pour half the chocolate filling into crust. Drop large spoonfuls of the peanut butter filling over the chocolate filling. Gently spoon remaining chocolate filling into pan. Drop spoonfuls of reserved peanut butter filling into pan. Cut through mixtures with knife for marble effect.
6. Bake in a preheated 300° oven for 45 to 55 minutes. Cheesecake is done when it springs back when lightly touched in the center (cheesecake will shake slightly when moved). Remove the cake from the oven and run a knife around the inside edge of pan.
7. Cool cheesecake on wire rack at room temperature for 1 hour. Cover pan with foil, then chill overnight. Serves 12 to 18.

Mint Chocolate Paisley Cheesecake

Crust:
2 cups chocolate cookie crumbs
1/4 cup margarine, melted
Filling:
3 8-ounce packages cream cheese, softened
2/3 cup sugar, scant
4 eggs
1 14-ounce can sweetened condensed milk
2 drops green food coloring
1 10-ounce package mint-chocolate chips, melted
Garnish:
1½ yards of 1-inch wide light green ribbon

1. In a small bowl stir together crust ingredients. Press firmly onto bottom and halfway up sides of a 9-inch springform pan.
2. In a large bowl using an electric mixer, beat cream cheese until light and fluffy. Gradually beat in sugar. Add eggs, one at a time, beating at low speed until blended. Add sweetened condensed milk, beating at low speed until well combined.
3. Transfer 1/3 cup filling to a small bowl. To this, stir in green food coloring. This green-tinted filling will be used to create the paisley design.
4. Add melted mint-chocolate chips to remaining filling. Beat with electric mixer at low speed until well combined. Pour mint-chocolate filling into crust.
5. Drop 6 spoonfuls of green-tinted filling over chocolate filling around edge of cheesecake, then drop 1 spoonful in the center. With a knife tip, pull a tail from each circle to simulate a paisley design.
6. Bake in a preheated 300° oven for 45 to 55 minutes. Cheesecake is done when it springs back when lightly touched in the center (cheesecake will shake slightly when moved). Remove the cake from the oven and run a knife around the inside edge of pan.
7. Cool cheesecake on wire rack at room temperature for 1 hour. Cover pan with foil, then chill overnight.
8. Garnish by tying a ribbon around the cheesecake. Serves 12 to 18.

Mint Marbled Cheesecake

Crust:
1½ cups chocolate cookie crumbs
3 tablespoons margarine, melted
Basic Filling:
3 8-ounce packages cream cheese, softened
1¼ cups sugar
3 eggs
1 cup sour cream
1 teaspoon vanilla extract
Mint Filling:
1¼ cups basic filling
1/4 teaspoon peppermint extract
2 drops green or red food coloring

1. In a small bowl stir together crust ingredients. Press firmly onto bottom of a 9-inch springform pan.
2. In a large bowl using an electric mixer, beat cream cheese until light and fluffy. Gradually beat in sugar. Add eggs, one at a time, beating at low speed until blended. Add sour cream and vanilla, beating at low speed until well combined.
3. For mint filling transfer 1¼ cups basic filling to a small bowl. To this, stir in peppermint extract and food coloring. Remove 1/2 cup mint filling and reserve. This will be used to create the marble design on the top of the cheesecake.
4. Pour half the basic filling into crust. Drop spoonfuls of mint filling over basic filling. Gently spoon remaining basic filling into pan. Drop spoonfuls of reserved mint filling into pan. Cut through mixtures with knife for marble effect.
5. Bake in a preheated 300° oven for 45 to 55 minutes. Cheesecake is done when it springs back when lightly touched in the center (cheesecake will shake slightly when moved). Remove the cake from the oven and run a knife around the inside edge of pan.
6. Cool cheesecake on wire rack at room temperature for 1 hour. Cover pan with foil, then chill overnight. Serves 12 to 18.

Mocha Marbled Cheesecake

Crust:
2 cups chocolate cookie crumbs
1/4 cup margarine, melted
Coffee Filling:
3 8-ounce packages cream cheese, softened
1¼ cups sugar
3 eggs
3 tablespoons Kahlúa
5 teaspoons instant coffee
1 cup sour cream
2 drops green food coloring
2 drops red food coloring
Mocha Filling:
1½ cups coffee filling
3 ounces semisweet chocolate, melted
3 tablespoons sugar

1. In a small bowl stir together crust ingredients. Press firmly onto bottom and halfway up sides of a 9-inch springform pan.
2. In a large bowl using an electric mixer, beat cream cheese until light and fluffy. Gradually beat in sugar. Add eggs, one at a time, beating at low speed until blended. Stir together Kahlúa and instant coffee. Add coffee mixture, sour cream, and food coloring to the cream cheese mixture. Beat at low speed until well combined.
3. For mocha filling transfer 1½ cups coffee filling to a small bowl. To this, stir in melted chocolate and sugar. Remove 1/2 cup mocha filling and reserve. This will be used to create the marble design on the top of the cheesecake.
4. Pour half the coffee filling into crust. Drop large spoonfuls of mocha filling over coffee filling. Gently spoon remaining coffee filling into pan. Drop spoonfuls of reserved mocha filling into pan. Cut through mixtures with knife for marble effect.
5. Bake in a preheated 300° oven for 45 to 55 minutes. Cheesecake is done when it springs back when lightly touched in the center (cheesecake will shake slightly when moved). Remove the cake from the oven and run a knife around the inside edge of pan.
6. Cool cheesecake on wire rack at room temperature for 1 hour. Cover pan with foil, then chill overnight. Serves 12 to 18.

★★★★★★★★★★★★★★★★★★★★★★★★

Raspberry Chocolate Marbled Cheesecake

Crust:
2 cups chocolate cookie crumbs
1/4 cup margarine, melted
Basic Filling:
3 8-ounce packages cream cheese, softened
4 eggs
1 14-ounce can sweetened condensed milk
2 tablespoons raspberry schnapps
1 teaspoon almond extract
Raspberry Filling:
2½ cups basic filling
1/2 cup red raspberry preserves
2 teaspoons flour
4 drops red food coloring
Chocolate Filling:
2½ cups basic filling
2 tablespoons sugar
2½ tablespoons sifted unsweetened cocoa powder

1. In a small bowl stir together crust ingredients. Press firmly onto bottom and halfway up sides of a 9-inch springform pan.
2. In a large bowl using an electric mixer, beat cream cheese until light and fluffy. Add eggs, one at a time, beating at low speed until blended. Add sweetened condensed milk, raspberry schnapps, and almond extract. Beat at low speed until well combined.
3. For raspberry filling transfer 2½ cups basic filling to a medium bowl. To this, stir in red raspberry preserves, flour, and red food coloring.
4. For chocolate filling add sugar and cocoa to remaining basic filling. Stir until well combined. Remove 1/2 cup chocolate filling and reserve. This will be used to create the marble design on the top of the cheesecake.
5. Pour half the raspberry filling into crust. Drop large spoonfuls of chocolate filling over the raspberry filling. Gently spoon the remaining raspberry filling into the pan. Drop spoonfuls of reserved chocolate filling into pan. Cut through mixtures with knife for marble effect.
6. Bake in a preheated 300° oven for 50 to 60 minutes. Cheesecake is done when it springs back when lightly touched in the center (cheesecake will shake slightly when moved). Remove the cake from the oven and run a knife around the inside edge of pan.

7. Cool cheesecake on wire rack at room temperature for 1 hour. Cover pan with foil, then chill overnight. Serves 12 to 18.

White Chocolate Lemon Marbled Cheesecake

Crust:
1 ¼ cups graham cracker crumbs
2 tablespoons sugar
3 tablespoons margarine, softened
Filling:
3 8-ounce packages cream cheese, softened
3/4 cup sugar
3 eggs
1/2 cup sour cream
1/3 cup lemon juice
12 ounces white chocolate, melted
1 tablespoon grated lemon rind
1/2 teaspoon almond extract
1/2 teaspoon lemon extract
1 teaspoon vanilla extract
3 drops yellow food coloring
Garnish:
5 stems of yellow silk flowers

1. In a small bowl stir together crust ingredients. Press firmly onto bottom of a 9-inch springform pan.
2. In a large bowl using an electric mixer, beat cream cheese until light and fluffy. Gradually beat in sugar. Add eggs, one at a time, beating at low speed until blended. Add sour cream, lemon juice, melted white chocolate, lemon rind, and extracts. Beat at low speed until well combined.
3. Transfer 1/2 cup filling to a small bowl. To this, stir in yellow food coloring.
4. Pour remaining filling into crust. Drop large spoonfuls of yellow mixture over white filling. Cut through mixtures with knife for marble effect.
5. Bake in a preheated 300° oven for 50 to 60 minutes. Cheesecake is done when it springs back when lightly touched in the center (cheesecake will shake slightly when moved). Remove the cake from the oven and run a knife around the inside edge of pan.
6. Cool cheesecake on wire rack at room temperature for 1 hour. Cover pan with foil, then chill overnight.
7. Place cheesecake on serving platter. Garnish by arranging silk flowers around base of cheesecake. Serves 12 to 18.

81

8
Peanut Butter Cheesecakes
★★★

Chocolate Peanut Butter Fudge Cheesecake

Crust:
3/4 cup graham cracker crumbs
3/4 cup chocolate cookie crumbs
1 tablespoon sugar
1/3 cup creamy peanut butter
2 tablespoons margarine, softened
Filling:
3 8-ounce packages cream cheese, softened
2/3 cup sugar
3/4 cup creamy peanut butter
4 eggs
1 14-ounce can sweetened condensed milk
1/4 cup sifted unsweetened cocoa powder
2 teaspoons vanilla extract

1. In a small bowl stir together crust ingredients. Press firmly onto bottom of a 9-inch springform pan.
2. In a large bowl using an electric mixer, beat cream cheese until light and fluffy. Gradually beat in sugar. Add peanut butter, beating until smooth. Add eggs, one at a time, beating at low speed until blended. Add remaining ingredients, beating at low speed until well combined. Pour mixture into crust.
3. Bake in a preheated 300° oven for 50 to 60 minutes. Cheesecake is done when it springs back when lightly touched in the center (cheesecake will shake slightly when moved). Remove the cake from the oven and run a knife around the inside edge of pan.
4. Cool cheesecake on wire rack at room temperature for 1 hour. Cover pan with foil, then chill overnight. Serves 12 to 18.

Peanut Butter Cheesecake

Crust:
2 cups graham cracker crumbs
1/4 cup sugar
1/4 cup margarine, softened
Filling:
2 8-ounce packages cream cheese, softened
3/4 cup sugar
1/3 cup creamy peanut butter
2 eggs
2/3 cup sour cream
1 teaspoon vanilla extract
Topping:
1½ cups sour cream
1/3 cup light brown sugar, packed
1 teaspoon vanilla extract

1. In a small bowl stir together crust ingredients. Press onto bottom and halfway up sides of a 9-inch springform pan.
2. In a large bowl using an electric mixer, beat cream cheese until light and fluffy. Gradually beat in sugar. Add peanut butter, beating until smooth. Add eggs one at a time, beating at low speed until blended. Add sour cream and vanilla, beating at low speed until well combined. Pour mixture into crust.
3. Bake in a preheated 300° oven for 45 to 55 minutes. Cheesecake is done when it springs back when lightly pressed in center (cheesecake will shake slightly when moved).
4. Remove the cake from the oven. In a small bowl stir together topping ingredients. Spread evenly over cheesecake. Return the cake to the oven for 3 to 5 minutes or until topping is set. Remove the cake from the oven and run a knife around the inside edge of pan.
5. Cool cheesecake on wire rack at room temperature for 1 hour. Cover pan with foil, then chill overnight. Serves 10 to 16.

PEANUT BUTTER CHEESECAKE WITH RASPBERRY SWIRL
Prepare the crust and filling as directed for Peanut Butter Cheesecake. Pour filling into crust. Pour 1/4 cup raspberry preserves into a decorator bag fitted with a large round tip. Pipe 6 to 7 parallel rows of preserves across filling. With knife tip, make 6 to 7 rows at right angle to the piped rows. Bake, cool, and chill as for Peanut Butter Cheesecake. Delete topping. Garnish edge with piped whipped cream, then sprinkle with chopped peanuts.

Peanut Butter Cup Cheesecake

Crust:
1½ cups chocolate cookie crumbs
3 tablespoons margarine, melted
Basic Filling:
3 8-ounce packages cream cheese, softened
4 eggs
1 14-ounce can sweetened condensed milk
2 teaspoons vanilla extract
Chocolate Filling:
2½ cups basic filling
1 cup semisweet chocolate chips, melted
1/3 cup sugar
Peanut Butter Filling:
2½ cups basic filling
1 cup creamy peanut butter
Glaze:
1 11½-ounce package milk chocolate chips
4 tablespoons milk

1. In a small bowl stir together crust ingredients. Press firmly onto bottom of an 8-inch springform pan.
2. In a large bowl using an electric mixer, beat cream cheese until light and fluffy. Add eggs, one at a time, beating at low speed until blended. Gradually add sweetened condensed milk and vanilla, beating at low speed until well combined.
3. For chocolate filling transfer 2½ cups basic filling to a medium bowl. To this, stir in melted chocolate chips and sugar. Reserve 1/3 cup chocolate filling. Pour remaining chocolate filling into crust.
4. For peanut butter filling add peanut butter to remaining basic filling. Using an electric mixer, beat at low speed until smooth. This is a very thick mixture. Holding the bowl about 2 feet over pan, quickly pour mixture into pan over chocolate filling. Pouring from this height pushes the batter in the center of the pan to the side, creating a cup-like design when the cake is cut.
5. Carefully spread the reserved 1/3 cup chocolate filling over the peanut butter filling. The chocolate filling is raised before baking, but it is level after baking.
6. Bake in a preheated 300° oven for 50 to 60 minutes. Cheesecake is done when it springs back when lightly touched in the center (cheesecake will shake slightly when moved). Remove the cake from the oven and run a knife around the inside edge of pan.
7. Cool cheesecake on wire rack at room temperature for 1 hour. Cover pan with foil, then chill overnight.

8. In a double boiler over hot, but not boiling water, place milk chocolate chips and milk. Melt, stirring constantly until smooth. Cool 10 minutes. Remove sides of pan. Spread glaze over top and sides of cake. Chill until topping is set, about 1 hour. Serves 12 to 18.

Triple Peanut Butter Cheesecake

Crust:
1½ cups graham cracker crumbs
2 tablespoons sugar
1/3 cup creamy peanut butter
2 tablespoons margarine, softened
Filling:
3 8-ounce packages cream cheese, softened
1¼ cups sugar
3 eggs
1 cup sour cream
2 teaspoons vanilla extract
1 cup peanut butter chips
Topping:
3 tablespoons creamy peanut butter
1/2 cup light brown sugar, packed
1 cup sour cream
1 teaspoon vanilla extract

1. In a small bowl stir together crust ingredients. Press firmly onto bottom of a 9-inch springform pan.
2. In a large bowl using an electric mixer, beat cream cheese until light and fluffy. Gradually beat in sugar. Add eggs, one at a time, beating at low speed until blended. Add sour cream and vanilla, beating at low speed until well combined.
3. Pour half the filling into the crust. Sprinkle with 1/2 cup peanut butter chips. Gently spoon remaining filling into pan. Sprinkle with remaining peanut butter chips.
4. Bake in a preheated 300° oven for 55 to 65 minutes. Cheesecake is done when it springs back when lightly touched in the center (cheesecake will shake slightly when moved).
4. Remove the cake from the oven. In a small bowl using an electric mixer, beat peanut butter with sugar. Add sour cream and vanilla. Spread evenly over cheesecake. Return the cake to the oven for 3 to 5 minutes or until topping is set. Remove the cake from the oven and run a knife around the inside edge of pan.
5. Cool cheesecake on wire rack at room temperature for 1 hour. Cover pan with foil, then chill overnight. Serves 12 to 18.

★★★★★★★★★★★★★★★★★★★★★★★

Peanut Butter Snickers Cheesecake

Crust:
1 ¼ cups graham cracker crumbs
2 tablespoons sugar
3 tablespoons margarine, softened
Filling:
2 8-ounce packages cream cheese, softened
2/3 cup sugar
1/3 cup creamy peanut butter
2 eggs
2/3 cup sour cream
1 teaspoon vanilla extract
1 ½ cups chopped Snickers candy bars
Glaze:
1 cup milk chocolate chips
2 tablespoons milk
Garnish:
Snickers candy bar, chopped

1. In a small bowl stir together crust ingredients. Press firmly onto bottom of a 9-inch springform pan.
2. In a large bowl using an electric mixer, beat cream cheese until light and fluffy. Gradually beat in sugar. Add peanut butter, beating until smooth. Add eggs, one at a time, beating at low speed until blended. Add sour cream and vanilla, beating at low speed until well combined.
3. Pour half the filling into crust. Sprinkle with half the chopped candy. Gently spoon remaining filling into pan. Sprinkle evenly with remaining chopped candy.
4. Bake in a preheated 300° oven for 50 to 60 minutes. Cheesecake is done when it springs back when lightly touched in the center (cheesecake will shake slightly when moved). Remove the cake from the oven and run a knife around the inside edge of pan.
5. Cool cheesecake on wire rack at room temperature for 1 hour. Cover pan with foil, then chill overnight.
6. In a double boiler over hot, but not boiling water, place milk chocolate chips and milk. Melt, stirring constantly until smooth. Cool 10 minutes. Remove sides of pan. Pour glaze over cheesecake, letting some drip off the sides. While glaze is still warm, sprinkle additional chopped candy evenly over cheesecake. Press to adhere. Chill until glaze is set, about 30 minutes. Serves 10 to 16.

Peanut Butter Fudge Cheesecake

Crust:
2 cups graham cracker crumbs
1/4 cup sugar
1/4 cup margarine, softened
Filling:
3 8-ounce packages cream cheese, softened
1/4 cup sugar
4 eggs
1 10-ounce package peanut butter chips
1/4 cup milk
1 14-ounce can sweetened condensed milk
1 teaspoon vanilla extract
Garnish:
Chocolate Drizzle (see page 16)

1. In a small bowl stir together crust ingredients. Press firmly onto bottom and halfway up sides of a 9-inch springform pan.
2. In a large bowl using an electric mixer, beat cream cheese until light and fluffy. Gradually beat in sugar. Add eggs, one at a time, beating at low speed until blended.
3. Place peanut butter chips and milk in a medium microwave-safe bowl. Microwave until melted. Stop and stir until mixture is smooth. Add melted peanut butter chip mixture, sweetened condensed milk, and vanilla to cream cheese mixture. Beat at low speed until well combined. Pour mixture into crust.
4. Bake in a preheated 300° oven for 50 to 60 minutes. Cheesecake is done when it springs back when lightly touched in the center (cheesecake will shake slightly when moved). Remove the cake from the oven and run a knife around the inside edge of pan.
5. Cool cheesecake on wire rack at room temperature for 1 hour. Cover pan with foil, then chill overnight.
6. Prepare Chocolate Drizzle. Place mixture in a decorator bag fitted with a round tip. Pipe a squiggle design over cheesecake. Chill until chocolate is set, about 15 minutes. Serves 12 to 18.

PEANUT BUTTER FUDGE CHOCOLATE CHIP CHEESECAKE
Prepare crust and filling as directed for Peanut Butter Fudge Cheesecake. Pour half the filling into crust. Sprinkle with 1/2 cup semisweet chocolate chips. Gently spoon the remaining filling into pan. Sprinkle with an additional 1/2 cup semisweet chocolate chips. Bake, cool, and chill as directed for Peanut Butter Fudge Cheesecake. Delete garnish.

9
Six-Inch Cheesecakes
★★★

Six-Inch Cheesecake

Crust:
1 cup graham cracker crumbs
1 tablespoon sugar
2 tablespoons margarine, softened
Filling:
1 8-ounce package cream cheese, softened
1/3 cup sugar
1 egg
1/3 cup sour cream
1 teaspoon vanilla extract

1. In a small bowl stir together crust ingredients. Press firmly onto bottom and halfway up sides of a 6-inch springform pan.
2. In a medium bowl using an electric mixer, beat cream cheese until light and fluffy. Gradually beat in sugar. Add egg, beating at low speed until blended. Add sour cream and vanilla, beating at low speed until well combined. Pour mixture into crust.
3. Bake in a preheated 300° oven for 50 to 60 minutes. Cheesecake is done when it springs back when lightly touched in the center (cheesecake will shake slightly when moved). Remove the cake from the oven and run a knife around the inside edge of pan.
4. Cool cheesecake on wire rack at room temperature for 1 hour. Cover pan with foil, then chill overnight. Serves 6.

Six-Inch Chocolate Cheesecake

Crust:
1 1/8 cups chocolate cookie crumbs
2 tablespoons margarine, melted
Filling:
1 8-ounce package cream cheese, softened
6 tablespoons sugar
1 egg

1/3 cup sour cream
1/3 cup semisweet chocolate chips, melted
1 teaspoon vanilla extract

1. In a small bowl stir together crust ingredients. Press firmly onto bottom and halfway up sides of a 6-inch springform pan.
2. In a medium bowl using an electric mixer, beat cream cheese until light and fluffy. Gradually beat in sugar. Add egg, beating at low speed until blended. Add remaining ingredients, beating at low speed until well combined. Pour mixture into crust.
3. Bake in a preheated 300° oven for 35 to 45 minutes. Cheesecake is done when it springs back when lightly touched in center (cheesecake will shake slightly when moved). Remove the cake from the oven and run a knife around the inside edge of pan.
4. Cool cheesecake on wire rack at room temperature for 1 hour. Cover pan with foil, then chill overnight. Serves 6.

Six-Inch Milk Chocolate Cheesecake

Crust:
1 cup graham cracker crumbs
1 tablespoon sugar
2 tablespoons margarine, softened
Filling:
1 8-ounce package cream cheese, softened
1/4 cup sugar
1 egg
1/3 cup sour cream
1/2 cup milk chocolate chips, melted
1 teaspoon vanilla extract

1. In a small bowl stir together crust ingredients. Press firmly onto bottom and halfway up sides of a 6-inch springform pan.
2. In a medium bowl using an electric mixer, beat cream cheese until light and fluffy. Gradually beat in sugar. Add egg, beating at low speed until blended. Add remaining ingredients, beating at low speed until well combined. Pour mixture into crust.
3. Bake in a preheated 300° oven for 30 to 40 minutes. Cheesecake is done when it springs back when lightly touched in center (cheesecake will shake slightly when moved). Remove the cake from the oven and run a knife around the inside edge of pan.
4. Cool cheesecake on wire rack at room temperature for 1 hour. Cover pan with foil, then chill overnight. Serves 6.

Sampler Cheesecake

Equipment:
3 6-inch springform pans
Crust:
3 cups graham cracker crumbs
3 tablespoons sugar
6 tablespoons margarine, softened
Basic Filling:
3 8-ounce packages cream cheese, softened
4 eggs
1 14-ounce can sweetened condensed milk
1 tablespoon vanilla extract
Chocolate Filling:
1 2/3 cups basic filling
3/4 cup semisweet chocolate chips, melted
2 tablespoons sugar
Butterscotch Filling:
1 2/3 cups basic filling
3/4 cup butterscotch chips, melted
Raspberry Filling:
1 2/3 cups basic filling
1/3 cup red raspberry preserves
2 teaspoons raspberry schnapps
1/2 teaspoon almond extract
3 drops red food coloring
Garnish:
9 chocolate leaves (see page 17)

1. In a small bowl stir together crust ingredients. Divide into 3 equal portions. Press firmly onto bottom and halfway up sides of 3 6-inch springform pans.
2. In a large bowl using an electric mixer, beat cream cheese until light and fluffy. Add eggs, one at a time, beating at low speed until blended. Add sweetened condensed milk and vanilla, beating at low speed until well combined. Divide batter into 3 equal portions, about 1 2/3 cups each. Transfer each portion to a separate bowl.
3. To each bowl, stir in all ingredients for the individual filling. Pour each mixture into a separate pan.
4. Place pans on large baking sheet. Bake in a preheated 300° oven for 45 to 55 minutes. Cheesecakes are done when they spring back when lightly touched in the center (cheesecakes will shake slightly when moved). Remove the cakes from the oven and run a knife around the inside edge of the pans.

★★★★★★★★★★ ★★★★★★★★★★★★ ★

5. Cool cheesecakes on wire rack at room temperature for 1 hour. Cover pans with foil, then chill overnight.
6. Cut each cheesecake into 6 equal portions. On 3 serving plates, assemble the slices by alternating flavors, using 2 slices from each cake. Garnish each cake with 3 chocolate leaves placed in the center. Yields 3 6-inch cheesecakes. Each cheesecake serves 6.

Petit Four Cheesecake

Crust:
1/2 cup chocolate cookie crumbs
1 tablespoon margarine, melted
Filling:
1 8-ounce package cream cheese, softened
1 egg
1/2 cup sweetened condensed milk
3/4 teaspoon almond extract
Glaze:
3 ounces semisweet chocolate
1 tablespoon butter
2 tablespoons milk
Garnish:
White Chocolate Drizzle (see page 16)

1. In a small bowl stir together crust ingredients. Press firmly onto bottom of a 6-inch springform pan.
2. In a medium bowl using an electric mixer, beat cream cheese until light and fluffy. Add egg, beating at low speed until blended. Add sweetened condensed milk and almond extract, beating at low speed until well combined. Pour mixture into crust.
3. Bake in preheated 300° oven for 20 to 30 minutes. Cheesecake is done when it springs back when lightly touched in the center (cheesecake will shake slightly when moved). Remove the cake from the oven and run a knife around the inside edge of pan.
4. Cool cheesecake on wire rack at room temperature for 1 hour. Cover pan with foil, then chill overnight.
5. Place chocolate, butter, and milk in a small microwave-safe bowl. Microwave until melted. Stop and stir until smooth. Cool 10 minutes. Blot cake to remove moisture. Place cake on rack with wax paper underneath. With knife, glaze top and sides of cake. Chill to set, about 30 minutes.
6. Place White Chocolate Drizzle in a small decorator bag fitted with a round tip. Pipe a border around the top edge of cake. Pipe dots on the top of the cake. Chill to set, about 15 minutes. Serves 6.

91

Birthday Cheesecake

Crust:
1 cup graham cracker crumbs
2 tablespoons sugar
2 teaspoons cocoa
2 tablespoons margarine, softened
Filling:
1 8-ounce package cream cheese, softened
1 egg
1/2 cup sweetened condensed milk
1 ounce semisweet chocolate, coarsely grated
3/4 teaspoon almond extract
Frosting:
3 ounces semisweet chocolate
1 tablespoon butter
1 tablespoon confectioners' sugar, sifted
2 tablespoons sour cream
1/4 teaspoon almond extract
Garnish:
Birthday candles

1. In a small bowl stir together crust ingredients. Press firmly onto bottom of a 6-inch springform pan.
2. In a medium bowl using an electric mixer, beat cream cheese until light and fluffy. Add egg, beating at low speed until blended. Add sweetened condensed milk, grated chocolate, and almond extract. Beat at low speed until well combined. Pour mixture into crust.
3. Bake in a preheated 300° oven for 20 to 30 minutes. Cheesecake is done when it springs back when lightly touched in the center (cheesecake will shake slightly when moved). Remove the cake from the oven and run a knife around the inside edge of pan.
4. Cool cheesecake on wire rack at room temperature for 1 hour. Cover pan with foil, then chill overnight.
5. Place chocolate and butter in a small microwave-safe bowl. Microwave until melted. Stop and stir until smooth. Stir in confectioners' sugar, sour cream, and almond extract. Frost top and sides of cheesecake. Arrange birthday candles around rim of cheesecake. Chill to set, about 30 minutes. Serves 6.

10
Special Cheesecakes
★★★

Butterscotch Cheesecake

Crust:
1 ¼ cups graham cracker crumbs
2 tablespoons light brown sugar, packed
3 tablespoons margarine, softened
Filling:
3 8-ounce packages cream cheese, softened
4 eggs
1 14-ounce can sweetened condensed milk
1 12-ounce package butterscotch chips, melted
2 teaspoons vanilla extract
Garnish:
8 to 10 butterscotch leaves (see page 17)

1. In a small bowl stir together crust ingredients. Press firmly onto bottom of
a 9-inch springform pan.
2. In a large bowl using an electric mixer, beat cream cheese until light and
fluffy. Add eggs, one at a time, beating at low speed until blended. Add
remaining filling ingredients, beating at low speed until well combined. Pour
mixture into crust.
3. Bake in a preheated 300° oven for 45 to 55 minutes. Cheesecake is done when
it springs back when lightly touched in the center (cheesecake will shake
slightly when moved). Remove the cake from the oven and run a knife around
the inside edge of pan.
4. Cool cheesecake on wire rack at room temperature for 1 hour. Cover pan
with foil, then chill overnight.
5. Garnish with butterscotch leaves. Serves 12 to 18.

★★★★★★★★★★★★★★★★★★★★★★★

Butterscotch Brownie Cheesecake

Crust:
2 cups graham cracker crumbs
1/4 cup sugar
1/4 cup margarine, softened
Filling:
3 8-ounce packages cream cheese, softened
1¼ cups light brown sugar, packed
3 eggs
1 cup sour cream
1 teaspoon vanilla extract
1 teaspoon imitation maple extract
2 cups of 1/2-inch cubed Butterscotch Brownies* (Freeze before cutting
   for best results.)

1. In a small bowl stir together crust ingredients. Press firmly onto bottom and
halfway up sides of a 9-inch springform pan.
2. In a large bowl using an electric mixer, beat cream cheese until light and
fluffy. Gradually beat in sugar. Add eggs, one at a time, beating at low speed
until blended. Add sour cream and extracts, beating at low speed until well
combined.
3. Pour one-third filling into crust. Sprinkle with one-third brownie cubes.
Gently spoon one-third filling into pan, then sprinkle again with one-third
brownie cubes. Gently spoon remaining filling into pan and sprinkle with
remaining brownie cubes. Press to make the top surface as even as possible.
4. Bake in preheated 300° oven for 45 to 55 minutes. Cheesecake is done when
it springs back when lightly touched in the center (cheesecake will shake
slightly when moved). Remove the cake from the oven and run a knife around
the inside edge of pan.
5. Cool cheesecake on wire rack at room temperature for 1 hour. Cover pan with
foil, then chill overnight. Serves 12 to 18.

*BUTTERSCOTCH BROWNIES
1 cup butterscotch chips
1/4 cup margarine
1 cup light brown sugar, packed
2 eggs
1 teaspoon vanilla extract
1 cup flour
1/2 teaspoon salt
1 teaspoon baking powder

94

1. Line a 9-inch square pan with foil. Grease the foil with shortening, then dust with flour.
2. In a double boiler over hot, but not boiling water, melt chips and margarine. Stir constantly until mixture is fairly smooth.
3. Transfer butterscotch-margarine mixture to a medium bowl. To this, stir in sugar. Add eggs and vanilla. Stir in flour, salt, and baking powder. Spread batter into pan.
4. Bake in a preheated 350° oven for 25 to 30 minutes. Brownies are done when a tester inserted in center comes out clean. Cool, then cut into 20 brownies. (Note: You will use 10 to 12 brownies for the cheesecake.)

Chocolate Chip Cookie Cheesecake

Crust:
2¼ cups chocolate chip cookie crumbs
3 tablespoons margarine, softened
Filling:
3 8-ounce packages cream cheese, softened
1¼ cups sugar
3 eggs
1 cup sour cream
2 teaspoons vanilla extract
1½ cups coarsely broken chocolate chip cookies

1. In a small bowl stir together crust ingredients. Press firmly onto bottom and halfway up sides of a 9-inch springform pan.
2. In a large bowl using an electric mixer, beat cream cheese until light and fluffy. Gradually beat in sugar. Add eggs, one at a time, beating at low speed until blended. Add sour cream and vanilla, beating at low speed until well combined.
3. Pour half the filling into crust. Sprinkle with 3/4 cup chocolate chip cookies. Gently spoon remaining filling into pan. Sprinkle evenly with remaining chocolate chip cookies.
4. Bake in a preheated 300° oven for 45 to 55 minutes. Cheesecake is done when it springs back when lightly touched in the center (cheesecake will shake slightly when moved). Remove the cake from the oven and run a knife around the inside edge of pan.
5. Cool cheesecake on wire rack at room temperature for 1 hour. Cover pan with foil, then chill overnight. Serves 12 to 18.

Carrot Cheesecake

Crust:
2 cups graham cracker crumbs
1/4 cup sugar
1 teaspoon cinnamon
1/4 cup margarine, softened
Filling:
3 8-ounce packages cream cheese, softened
1 ¼ cups sugar
3 eggs
1 cup sour cream
1 cup finely shredded carrot
1 8 ¼-ounce can crushed pineapple in syrup, well drained
1 teaspoon cinnamon
2 tablespoons Curaçao
2 teaspoons vanilla extract
1 drop red food coloring
1 drop yellow food coloring
1/2 cup raisins

1. In a small bowl stir together crust ingredients. Press firmly onto bottom and halfway up sides of a 9-inch springform pan.
2. In a large bowl using an electric mixer, beat cream cheese until light and fluffy. Gradually beat in sugar. Add eggs, one at a time, beating at low speed until blended. Add sour cream, carrot, pineapple, cinnamon, Curaçao, vanilla, and food coloring. Beat at low speed until well combined.
3. Pour half the filling into crust. Sprinkle with 1/4 cup raisins. Gently spoon remaining filling into pan. Sprinkle with remaining raisins.
4. Bake in a preheated 300° oven for 50 to 60 minutes. Cheesecake is done when it springs back when lightly touched in center (cheesecake will shake slightly when moved). Remove the cake from the oven and run a knife around the inside edge of pan.
5. Cool cheesecake on wire rack at room temperature for 1 hour. Cover pan with foil, then chill overnight. Serves 12 to 18.

Chocolate Chip Walnut Cheesecake

Crust:
3/4 cup chocolate cookie crumbs
3/4 cup graham cracker crumbs
1/2 cup chopped walnuts
2 tablespoons sugar
1/4 cup margarine, melted
Filling:
3 8-ounce packages cream cheese, softened
1¼ cups sugar
3 eggs
1 cup sour cream
2 teaspoons imitation walnut extract, heaping
1 cup semisweet chocolate chips
2/3 cup coarsely chopped walnuts
Garnish:
Whipped cream
Walnut halves
Chocolate syrup

1. In a small bowl stir together crust ingredients. Press firmly onto bottom and halfway up sides of a 9-inch springform pan.
2. In a large bowl using an electric mixer, beat cream cheese until light and fluffy. Gradually beat in sugar. Add eggs, one at a time, beating at low speed until blended. Add sour cream and walnut extract, beating at low speed until well combined.
3. Pour half the filling into crust. Sprinkle with 1/2 cup chocolate chips and 1/3 cup chopped walnuts. Gently spoon remaining filling into pan. Sprinkle evenly with remaining chocolate chips and chopped walnuts.
4. Bake in a preheated 300° oven for 55 to 65 minutes. Cheesecake is done when it springs back when lightly touched in the center (cheesecake will shake slightly when moved). Remove the cake from the oven and run a knife around the inside edge of pan.
5. Cool cheesecake on wire rack at room temperature for 1 hour. Cover pan with foil, then chill overnight.
6. Garnish edge of cheesecake with dollops of whipped cream. Stud each dollop with a walnut half. Drizzle chocolate syrup over walnut and cream. Serves 12 to 18.

Eggnog Cheesecake

Crust:
2 cups graham cracker crumbs
1/4 cup sugar
1/4 cup margarine, softened
Filling:
3 8-ounce packages cream cheese, softened
1¼ cups sugar
3 eggs
1 cup sour cream
1½ teaspoons nutmeg
2 tablespoons dark rum
1 teaspoon vanilla extract
1½ teaspoons imitation rum extract
Topping:
1 1/3 cups sour cream
2 tablespoons sugar
1/8 teaspoon nutmeg
2 tablespoons dark rum
Garnish:
Nutmeg

1. In a small bowl stir together crust ingredients. Press firmly onto bottom and halfway up sides of a 9-inch springform pan.
2. In a large bowl using an electric mixer, beat cream cheese until light and fluffy. Gradually beat in sugar. Add eggs, one at a time, beating at low speed until blended. Add remaining filling ingredients, beating at low speed until well combined. Pour mixture into crust.
3. Bake in a preheated 300° oven for 1 hour to 1 hour and 10 minutes. Cheesecake is done when it springs back when lightly touched in center (cheesecake will shake slightly when moved).
4. Remove the cake from the oven. In a small bowl stir together topping ingredients. Spread evenly over cheesecake. Return the cake to the oven for 3 to 5 minutes or until topping is set. Remove the cake from the oven and run a knife around the inside edge of the pan.
5. Cool cheesecake on wire rack at room temperature for 1 hour. Cover pan with foil, then chill overnight.
6. Garnish with a sprinkle of nutmeg. Serves 12 to 18.

Greek Cheesecake

Crust:
1½ cups graham cracker crumbs
1/2 cup finely chopped walnuts
1/4 cup sugar
1/4 cup margarine, softened
Filling:
2 8-ounce packages cream cheese, softened
1/2 cup honey
2 eggs
1/2 cup sour cream
2 teaspoons lemon juice
1/2 teaspoon grated lemon rind
1 teaspoon vanilla extract
Garnish:
2 to 3 tablespoons finely chopped walnuts
1 lemon slice twist (see page 17)

1. In a small bowl stir together crust ingredients. Press firmly onto bottom and halfway up sides of a 9-inch springform pan.
2. In a large bowl using an electric mixer, beat cream cheese until light and fluffy. Gradually beat in honey. Add eggs, one at a time, beating at low speed until blended. Add remaining filling ingredients, beating at low speed until well combined. Pour mixture into crust.
3. Bake in a preheated 300° oven for 40 to 50 minutes. Cheesecake is done when the filling is set. (The batter is sticky. Unlike other cheesecakes when done, the batter will stick to your finger when pressed in the center.) Remove the cake from the oven and run a knife around the inside edge of the pan.
4. Cool cheesecake on wire rack at room temperature for 1 hour. Cover pan with foil, then chill overnight.
5. Sprinkle finely chopped walnuts around the edge of the cheesecake. Place a lemon slice twist in the center. Serves 10 to 16.

Italian Cheesecake

Crust:
1½ cups flour
1/3 cup sugar
1 large egg, separated
1/2 cup butter, softened
1 teaspoon grated lemon rind
1/4 teaspoon almond extract
Filling:
1/3 cup dark rum
1/2 cup golden raisins
3 3/4 cups ricotta cheese, drained
1 cup sugar
4 eggs
1 tablespoon cornstarch
1 teaspoon grated orange rind
1 teaspoon almond extract
1 teaspoon vanilla extract
1/2 cup sliced almonds
Garnish:
1 to 2 tablespoons golden raisins
1 to 2 tablespoons sliced almonds
Confectioners' sugar

1. In a small bowl stir together flour and sugar. Using your hand, add egg yolk, softened butter, lemon rind, and almond extract. Shape dough into a ball. Remove sides of a 9-inch springform pan. Using your fingers press half the dough onto bottom of pan. Bake in a preheated 400° oven for 10 to 15 minutes or until light brown. Cool. Attach side of pan to bottom. Using your fingers press remaining dough onto sides of pan. Make sure that the side crust meets the bottom crust all the way around. Brush the reserved egg white on the side and the bottom. This seals the crust and prevents it from becoming soggy.
2. In a small saucepan heat dark rum until hot, but not boiling. Stir in raisins; remove from heat. Let plump for 20 minutes. Drain the raisins, discarding the rum.
3. In a large bowl with a wooden spoon stir together the ricotta and sugar. Add the eggs, cornstarch, orange rind, and extracts. Stir in drained raisins and sliced almonds. Pour mixture into cooled crust.
4. Bake in a preheated 325° oven for 1 hour. This cheesecake is baked at a higher temperature than the other recipes. The cheesecake is done when the filling is firm.

5. Cool on wire rack at room temperature for 1 hour. Cover pan with foil, then chill overnight.
6. Garnish with golden raisins and sliced almonds. Sprinkle with confectioners' sugar. Serves 12 to 18.

Maple Pecan Cheesecake

Crust:
1½ cups graham cracker crumbs
1/2 cup finely chopped pecans, toasted
1/4 cup sugar
1/4 cup margarine, softened
Filling:
3 8-ounce packages cream cheese, softened
1¼ cups light brown sugar, packed
3 eggs
1 cup sour cream
2 teaspoons imitation maple extract, heaping
1 cup chopped pecans, toasted
2 tablespoons light brown sugar
Garnish:
Pecan halves

1. In a small bowl stir together crust ingredients. Press firmly onto bottom and halfway up sides of a 9-inch springform pan.
2. In a large bowl using an electric mixer, beat cream cheese until light and fluffy. Gradually beat in sugar. Add eggs, one at a time, beating at low speed until blended. Add sour cream and maple extract, beating at low speed until well combined.
3. Pour half the filling into crust. Sprinkle with 1/2 cup pecans. Gently spoon remaining filling into pan. Sprinkle with remaining pecans and 2 tablespoons light brown sugar.
4. Bake in a preheated 300° oven for 50 to 60 minutes. Cheesecake is done when it springs back when lightly touched in the center (cheesecake will shake slightly when moved). Remove the cake from the oven and run a knife around the inside edge of the pan.
5. Cool cheesecake on wire rack at room temperature for 1 hour. Cover pan with foil, then chill overnight.
6. Garnish cheesecake with pecan halves placed around edge. Serves 12 to 18.

Peppermint Chocolate Chip Cheesecake

Crust:
1½ cups chocolate cookie crumbs
3 tablespoons margarine, melted
Filling:
3 8-ounce packages cream cheese, softened
1¼ cups sugar
3 eggs
1 cup sour cream
1 teaspoon peppermint extract
5 drops red food coloring
1 1/3 cups semisweet chocolate chips
Garnish:
Whipped cream
Chocolate chips

1. In a small bowl stir together crust ingredients. Press firmly onto bottom of a 9-inch springform pan.
2. In a large bowl using an electric mixer, beat cream cheese until light and fluffy. Gradually beat in sugar. Add eggs, one at a time, beating at low speed until blended. Add sour cream, peppermint extract, and food coloring. Beat at low speed until well combined.
3. Pour one-third filling into crust. Sprinkle with one-third of the chocolate chips. Gently spoon one-third filling into pan, then sprinkle again with one-third of the chocolate chips. Gently spoon remaining filling into pan and sprinkle with remaining chocolate chips.
4. Bake in preheated 300° oven for 50 to 60 minutes. Cheesecake is done when it springs back when lightly touched in the center (cheesecake will shake slightly when moved). Remove the cake from the oven and run a knife around the inside edge of pan.
5. Cool cheesecake on wire rack at room temperature for 1 hour. Cover pan with foil, then chill overnight.
6. Garnish edge of cheesecake with dollops of whipped cream. Sprinkle chocolate chips over whipped cream. Serves 12 to 18.

Pumpkin Cheesecake

Crust:
2 cups graham cracker crumbs
1/4 cup sugar
1 teaspoon cinnamon
1/4 cup margarine, softened
Filling:
3 8-ounce packages cream cheese, softened
1 cup light brown sugar, packed
1/2 cup sugar
4 eggs
1/2 cup sour cream
1 cup canned pumpkin
2 teaspoons cinnamon
1 teaspoon cloves
1 teaspoon ginger
1 tablespoon vanilla extract
2 teaspoons imitation maple extract
Garnish:
White Chocolate Drizzle (see page 16)

1. In a small bowl stir together crust ingredients. Press firmly onto bottom and
halfway up sides of a 9-inch springform pan.
2. In a large bowl using an electric mixer, beat cream cheese until light and
fluffy. Gradually beat in sugars. Add eggs, one at a time, beating at low speed
until blended. Add remaining filling ingredients, beating at low speed until
well combined. Pour mixture into crust.
3. Bake in a preheated 300° oven for 1 hour and 20 minutes to 1 hour
and 30 minutes. Cheesecake is done when it springs back when lightly touched
in the center (cheesecake is very wobbly when moved). Remove the cake from
the oven and run a knife around the inside edge of pan.
4. Cool cheesecake on wire rack at room temperature for 1 hour. Cover pan
with foil, then chill overnight.
5. Prepare White Chocolate Drizzle. Pour mixture into a decorator bag fitted
with a round tip. Pipe a lattice design over cake. Serves 12 to 18.

Sweet Potato Cheesecake

Crust:
2 cups graham cracker crumbs
1/4 cup sugar
1 teaspoon cinnamon
1/4 cup margarine, softened
Filling:
3 8-ounce packages cream cheese, softened
1 cup light brown sugar, packed
1/2 cup sugar
4 eggs
1/2 cup sour cream
1 cup mashed sweet potato, room temperature
1 teaspoon cinnamon
1/2 teaspoon ginger
1 tablespoon vanilla extract
4 drops red food coloring
4 drops green food coloring
Garnish:
1½ to 2 cups miniature marshmallows

1. In a small bowl stir together crust ingredients. Press firmly onto bottom and halfway up sides of a 9-inch springform pan.
2. In a large bowl using an electric mixer, beat cream cheese until light and fluffy. Gradually beat in sugars. Add eggs, one at a time, beating at low speed until blended. Add remaining filling ingredients, beating at low speed until well combined. Pour mixture into crust.
3. Bake in a preheated 300° oven for 1 hour to 1 hour and 10 minutes. Cheesecake is done when it springs back when lightly touched in the center (cheesecake will shake slightly when moved). Remove the cake from the oven and run a knife around the inside edge of the pan.
4. Cool cheesecake on wire rack at room temperature for 1 hour. Cover pan with foil, then chill overnight.
5. Sprinkle miniature marshmallows over cheesecake. Broil until miniature marshmallows are lightly toasted. Serve immediately. Serves 12 to 18.

Toffee Cheesecake

Crust:
1 cup chocolate cookie crumbs
1 cup graham cracker crumbs
1/4 cup margarine, melted
Filling:
3 8-ounce packages cream cheese, softened
3 eggs
1 14-ounce can sweetened condensed milk
3 ounces unsweetened chocolate, melted
1½ cups butterscotch chips, melted
1 teaspoon vanilla extract
Garnish:
Chocolate leaves (see page 17)
Butterscotch leaves (see page 17)

1. In a small bowl stir together crust ingredients. Press firmly onto bottom and halfway up sides of a 9-inch springform pan.
2. In a large bowl using an electric mixer, beat cream cheese until light and fluffy. Add eggs, one at a time, beating at low speed until blended. Add remaining filling ingredients, beating at low speed until well combined. Pour mixture into crust.
3. Bake in a preheated 300° oven for 45 to 55 minutes. Cheesecake is done when it springs back when lightly touched in the center (cheesecake will shake slightly when moved). Remove the cake from the oven and run a knife around the inside edge of pan.
4. Cool cheesecake on wire rack at room temperature for 1 hour. Cover pan with foil, then chill overnight.
5. Garnish with chocolate and butterscotch leaves. Serves 12 to 18.

Trifle Cheesecake

Crust:
1 ¼ cups graham cracker crumbs
2 tablespoons sugar
3 tablespoons margarine, softened
Filling:
3 8-ounce packages cream cheese, softened
3 eggs
1 14-ounce can sweetened condensed milk
2 teaspoons vanilla extract
1/2 teaspoon almond extract
2 cups cubed angel food cake, heaping
1/4 cup dark rum
1/2 cup red raspberry preserves
1/2 cup sliced almonds
Garnish:
1/2 cup red raspberry preserves
Whipped cream
Sliced almonds
Maraschino cherries, halved and drained

1. In a small bowl stir together crust ingredients. Press firmly onto bottom of
a 9-inch springform pan.
2. In a large bowl using an electric mixer, beat cream cheese until light and
fluffy. Add eggs, one at a time, beating at low speed until blended. Add
sweetened condensed milk and extracts, beating at low speed until well
combined. Pour half the mixture into crust.
3. In a medium bowl stir together cake cubes and rum, tossing to coat
thoroughly. Sprinkle cake cubes evenly into pan.
4. Heat raspberry preserves, stirring until smooth. Spread over cake cubes.
Sprinkle with sliced almonds. Gently spoon remaining filling into pan. Some of
the cake cubes will float to the surface.
5. Bake in a preheated 300° oven for 40 to 50 minutes. Cheesecake is done
when it springs back when lightly touched in the center (cheesecake will
shake slightly when moved). Remove the cake from the oven and run a knife
around the inside edge of pan.
6. Cool cheesecake on wire rack at room temperature for 1 hour. Cover pan
with foil, then chill overnight.
7. Heat 1/2 cup raspberry preserves, stirring until smooth. Spread evenly over
cake. Spread whipped cream over preserves to cover. Garnish with sliced
almonds and maraschino cherries. Serves 12 to 18.

11
Spirited Cheesecakes
★★★

Chocolate Hazelnut Cheesecake

Crust:
2 cups graham cracker crumbs
1/4 cup sugar
1/4 cup margarine, softened
Filling:
3 8-ounce packages cream cheese, softened
1 ¼ cups sugar
3 eggs
3/4 cup sour cream
1 cup semisweet chocolate chips, melted
1/2 cup hazelnut schnapps
1 teaspoon cinnamon
2 teaspoons vanilla extract
Garnish:
Chopped hazelnuts

1. In a small bowl stir together crust ingredients. Press firmly onto bottom
and halfway up sides of a 9-inch springform pan.
2. In a large bowl using an electric mixer, beat cream cheese until light and
fluffy. Gradually beat in sugar. Add eggs, one at a time, beating at low
speed until blended. Add remaining filling ingredients, beating until well
combined. Pour mixture into crust.
3. Bake in a preheated 300° oven for 50 to 60 minutes. Cheesecake is done when
it springs back when lightly touched in the center (cheesecake will shake slightly
when moved). Remove the cake from the oven and run a knife around the inside
edge of pan.
4. Cool cheesecake on rack at room temperature for 1 hour. Cover pan
with foil, then chill overnight.
5. Garnish edge of cheesecake with chopped hazelnuts. Serves 12 to 18.

★★★★★★★★★★★★★★★★★★★★★

Amaretto Marzipan Cheesecake

Crust:
2 cups graham cracker crumbs
1/4 cup sugar
1/4 cup margarine, softened
Filling:
1 7-ounce package almond paste
1 cup sugar
10 tablespoons amaretto
3 8-ounce packages cream cheese, softened
3 eggs
1/2 cup sour cream
1 teaspoon almond extract
Topping:
1 1/3 cups sour cream
2 tablespoons sugar
2 tablespoons amaretto
Garnish:
Stemmed maraschino cherries, drained
White chocolate leaves (see page 17)

1. In a small bowl stir together crust ingredients. Press firmly onto bottom and halfway up sides of a 9-inch springform pan.
2. Crumble almond paste into a small bowl. Add sugar, mixing by hand until of even consistency. Using an electric mixer at low speed, beat in amaretto. Gradually increase speed from medium to high, beating until mixture is smooth.
3. In a large bowl using an electric mixer, beat cream cheese until light and fluffy. Gradually add almond paste mixture to cream cheese, beating until smooth. Add eggs, one at a time, beating at low speed until blended. Add sour cream and almond extract, beating at low speed until well combined. Pour mixture into crust.
4. Bake in a preheated 300° oven for 1 hour to 1 hour and 10 minutes. Cheesecake is done when it springs back when lightly touched in the center (cheesecake is very wobbly when moved).
5. Remove the cake from the oven. In a small bowl stir together topping ingredients. Spread evenly over cheesecake. Return the cake to the oven

for 3 to 5 minutes to set topping. Remove the cake from the oven and run a knife around the inside edge of pan.

6. Cool cheesecake on wire rack at room temperature for 1 hour. Cover pan with foil, then chill overnight.

7. Garnish center of cheesecake with cherries surrounded by white chocolate leaves. Serves 12 to 18.

Crème de Menthe Cheesecake

Crust:
1½ cups chocolate cookie crumbs
3 tablespoons margarine, melted
Filling:
3 8-ounce packages cream cheese, softened
1 cup sugar
3 eggs
3/4 cup sour cream
6 tablespoons crème de menthe liqueur
Garnish:
Whipped cream
Mint leaves

1. In a small bowl stir together crust ingredients. Press firmly onto bottom of a 9-inch springform pan.

2. In a large bowl using an electric mixer, beat cream cheese until light and fluffy. Gradually beat in sugar. Add eggs, one at a time, beating at low speed until blended. Add sour cream and crème de menthe liqueur, beating at low speed until well combined. Pour mixture into crust.

3. Bake in a preheated 300° oven for 50 to 60 minutes. Cheesecake is done when it springs back when lightly touched in the center (cheesecake will shake slightly when moved). Remove the cake from the oven and run a knife around the inside edge of pan.

4. Cool cheesecake on wire rack at room temperature for 1 hour. Cover pan with foil, then chill overnight.

5. Garnish individual slices with a dollop of whipped cream. Stud each dollop with a mint leaf. Serves 12 to 18.

Black Forest Cheesecake

Crust:
1½ cups chocolate cookie crumbs
3 tablespoons margarine, melted
Filling:
3 8-ounce packages cream cheese, softened
1 cup sugar
3 eggs
1/2 cup sour cream
1 12-ounce package semisweet chocolate chips, melted
3/4 cup Cherry Herring liqueur
1 teaspoon vanilla extract
Garnish:
Cherry pie filling
Whipped cream
Coarsely grated chocolate

1. In a small bowl stir together crust ingredients. Press firmly onto bottom of a 9-inch springform pan.
2. In a large bowl using an electric mixer, beat cream cheese until light and fluffy. Gradually beat in sugar. Add eggs, one at a time, beating at low speed until blended. Add remaining filling ingredients, beating at low speed until well combined. Pour mixture into crust.
3. Bake in a preheated 300° oven for 55 to 65 minutes. Cheesecake is done when it springs back when lightly touched in the center (cheesecake will shake slightly when moved). Remove the cake from the oven and run a knife around the inside edge of pan.
4. Cool cheesecake on wire rack at room temperature for 1 hour. Cover pan with foil, then chill overnight.
5. Garnish with cherry pie filling spread evenly over top of cheesecake, leaving an 1-inch margin around the edge. Spread whipped cream on sides of cheesecake and in the 1-inch margin on the top of the cheesecake. Press grated chocolate into the whipped cream. Serves 12 to 18.

Black Russian Cheesecake

Crust:
2 cups graham cracker crumbs
1/4 cup sugar
1/4 cup margarine, softened
Filling:
3 8-ounce packages cream cheese, softened
1 cup sugar
3 eggs
3/4 cup sour cream
5 tablespoons Kahlúa
1/4 cup vodka
2 teaspoons vanilla extract
2 drops red food coloring
2 drops green food coloring
Topping:
1 1/3 cups sour cream
2 tablespoons sugar
1 tablespoon Kahlúa
1 tablespoon vodka
Garnish:
Chocolate curls

1. In a small bowl stir together crust ingredients. Press firmly onto bottom and halfway up sides of a 9-inch springform pan.
2. In a large bowl using an electric mixer, beat cream cheese until light and fluffy. Gradually beat in sugar. Add eggs, one at a time, beating at low speed until blended. Add remaining filling ingredients, beating at low speed until well combined. Pour mixture into crust.
3. Bake in a preheated 300° oven for 50 to 60 minutes. Cheesecake is done when it springs back when lightly touched in the center (cheesecake will shake slightly when moved).
4. Remove the cake from the oven. In a small bowl stir together topping ingredients. Spread evenly over cheesecake. Return the cake to the oven for 3 to 5 minutes or until topping is set. Remove the cake from the oven and run a knife around the inside edge of pan.
5. Cool cheesecake on wire rack at room temperature for 1 hour. Cover pan with foil, then chill overnight.
6. Garnish cheesecake with chocolate curls. Serves 12 to 18.

★★★★★★★★★★★★★★★★★★★★★★★★★

Brandy Alexander Cheesecake

Crust:
1 ¼ cups graham cracker crumbs
2 tablespoons sugar
3 tablespoons margarine, softened
Filling:
3 8-ounce packages cream cheese, softened
1 cup sugar
3 eggs
3/4 cup sour cream
1 tablespoon sifted unsweetened cocoa powder
5 tablespoons brandy
5 tablespoons white crème de cacao
2 teaspoons vanilla extract
5 to 6 drops green food coloring
5 to 6 drops red food coloring
Topping:
1 1/3 cups sour cream
2 tablespoons sugar
1 tablespoon brandy
1 tablespoon white crème de cacao
Garnish:
White chocolate leaves (see page 17)

1. In a small bowl stir together crust ingredients. Press firmly onto bottom of a 9-inch springform pan.
2. In a large bowl using an electric mixer, beat cream cheese until light and fluffy. Gradually beat in sugar. Add eggs, one at a time, beating at low speed until blended. Add remaining filling ingredients, beating at low speed until well combined. Pour mixture into crust.
3. Bake in a preheated 300° oven for 50 to 60 minutes. Cheesecake is done when it springs back when lightly touched in the center (cheesecake will shake slightly when moved).
4. Remove the cake from the oven. In a small bowl stir together topping ingredients. Spread evenly over cheesecake. Return the cake to the oven for 3 to 5 minutes to set topping. Remove the cake from the oven and run a knife around the inside edge of pan.
5. Cool cheesecake on wire rack at room temperature for 1 hour. Cover pan with foil, then chill overnight.
6. Garnish cheesecake with white chocolate leaves. Serves 12 to 18.

Chocolate Amaretto Cheesecake

Crust:
2 cups chocolate cookie crumbs
1/4 cup margarine, melted
Filling:
3 8-ounce packages cream cheese, softened
3/4 cup sugar
3 eggs
1/2 cup sour cream
1 11½-ounce package milk chocolate chips, melted
3/4 cup amaretto
1 teaspoon vanilla extract
Topping:
1 1/3 cups sour cream
2 tablespoons sugar
2 tablespoons amaretto
Garnish:
Sliced almonds

1. In a small bowl stir together crust ingredients. Press firmly onto bottom and halfway up sides of a 9-inch springform pan.
2. In a large bowl using an electric mixer, beat cream cheese until light and fluffy. Gradually beat in sugar. Add eggs, one at a time, beating at low speed until blended. Add remaining filling ingredients, beating at low speed until well combined. Pour mixture into crust.
3. Bake in a preheated 300° oven for 55 to 65 minutes. Cheesecake is done when it springs back when lightly touched in the center (cheesecake will shake slightly when moved).
4. Remove the cake from the oven. In a small bowl stir together topping ingredients. Spread evenly over cheesecake. Return the cake to the oven for 3 to 5 minutes or until topping is set. Remove the cake from the oven and run a knife around the inside edge of the pan.
5. Cool cheesecake on wire rack at room temperature for 1 hour. Cover pan with foil, then chill overnight.
6. Garnish with sliced almonds. Serves 12 to 18.

Crème de Cacao Cheesecake

Crust:
1½ cups chocolate cookie crumbs
3 tablespoons margarine, melted
Filling:
3 8-ounce packages cream cheese, softened
1¼ cups sugar
3 eggs
3/4 cup sour cream
1/2 cup crème de cacao
1 cup semisweet chocolate chips, melted
2 teaspoons vanilla extract
Garnish:
Chocolate leaves (see page 17)
Confectioners' sugar

1. In a small bowl stir together crust ingredients. Press firmly onto bottom of a 9-inch springform pan.
2. In a large bowl using an electric mixer, beat cream cheese until light and fluffy. Gradually beat in sugar. Add eggs, one at a time, beating at low speed until blended. Add remaining filling ingredients, beating at low speed until well combined. Pour mixture into crust.
3. Bake in a preheated 300° oven for 40 to 50 minutes. Cheesecake is done when it springs back when lightly touched in the center (cheesecake will shake slightly when moved). Remove the cake from the oven and run a knife around the inside edge of pan.
4. Cool cheesecake on wire rack at room temperature for 1 hour. Cover pan with foil, then chill overnight.
5. Garnish with chocolate leaves, then sprinkle with confectioners' sugar.
Serves 12 to 18.

Curaçao Cheesecake

Crust:
2 cups graham cracker crumbs
1/4 cup sugar
1/4 cup margarine, softened
Filling:
3 8-ounce packages cream cheese, softened
1 cup light brown sugar, packed
3 eggs
3/4 cup sour cream
1/2 cup Curaçao
2 teaspoons vanilla extract
8 drops red food coloring
8 drops yellow food coloring
Garnish:
Confectioners' sugar
Orange slice twist (see page 17)

1. In a small bowl stir together crust ingredients. Press firmly onto bottom and halfway up sides of a 9-inch springform pan.
2. In a large bowl using an electric mixer, beat cream cheese until light and fluffy. Gradually beat in sugar. Add eggs, one at a time, beating at low speed until blended. Add remaining filling ingredients, beating at low speed until well combined. Pour mixture into crust.
3. Bake in a preheated 300° oven for 50 to 60 minutes. Cheesecake is done when it springs back when lightly touched in the center (cheesecake will shake slightly when moved). Remove the cake from the oven and run a knife around the inside edge of pan.
4. Cool cheesecake on wire rack at room temperature for 1 hour. Cover pan with foil, then chill overnight.
5. Blot cake, then sprinkle with confectioners' sugar. Garnish with an orange slice twist. Serves 12 to 18.

Grasshopper Cheesecake

Crust:
2 cups chocolate cookie crumbs
1/4 cup margarine, melted
Filling:
3 8-ounce packages cream cheese, softened
1 cup sugar
3 eggs
3/4 cup sour cream
6 tablespoons crème de menthe liqueur
3 tablespoons white crème de cacao
Garnish:
Whipped cream
Chocolate leaves (see page 17)

1. In a small bowl stir together crust ingredients. Press firmly onto bottom and halfway up sides of a 9-inch springform pan.
2. In a large bowl using an electric mixer, beat cream cheese until light and fluffy. Gradually beat in sugar. Add eggs, one at a time, beating at low speed until blended. Add remaining filling ingredients, beating at low speed until well combined. Pour mixture into crust.
3. Bake in a preheated 300° oven for 50 to 60 minutes. Cheesecake is done when it springs back when lightly touched in the center (cheesecake will shake slightly when moved). Remove the cake from the oven and run a knife around the inside edge of pan.
4. Cool cheesecake on wire rack at room temperature for 1 hour. Cover pan with foil, then chill overnight.
5. Garnish with dollops of whipped cream around the edge of the cheesecake. Stud each dollop with a chocolate leaf. Serves 12 to 18.

Hazelnut Cheesecake

Crust:
1½ cups graham cracker crumbs
3/4 cup ground hazelnuts
2 tablespoons sugar
2 tablespoons margarine, melted
Filling:
3 8-ounce packages cream cheese, softened
1 cup sugar
3 eggs
3/4 cup sour cream
1/2 cup hazelnut schnapps
2 drops red food coloring
4 drops yellow food coloring
Topping:
1 1/3 cups sour cream
2 tablespoons sugar
2 tablespoons hazelnut schnapps
Garnish:
Chopped hazelnuts

1. In a small bowl stir together crust ingredients. Press firmly onto bottom and halfway up sides of a 9-inch springform pan.
2. In a large bowl using an electric mixer, beat cream cheese until light and fluffy. Gradually beat in sugar. Add eggs, one at a time, beating at low speed until blended. Add remaining filling ingredients, beating at low speed until well combined. Pour mixture into crust.
3. Bake in a preheated 300° oven for 45 to 55 minutes. Cheesecake is done when it springs back when lightly touched in the center (cheesecake will shake slightly when moved).
4. Remove the cake from the oven. In a small bowl stir together topping ingredients. Spread evenly over cheesecake. Return the cake to the oven for 3 to 5 minutes or until topping is set. Remove the cake from the oven and run a knife around the inside edge of pan.
5. Cool cheesecake on wire rack at room temperature for 1 hour. Cover pan with foil, then chill overnight.
6. Garnish with chopped hazelnuts. Serves 12 to 18.

Irish Cream Cheesecake

Crust:
2 cups graham cracker crumbs
1/4 cup sugar
1/4 cup margarine, softened
Filling:
3 8-ounce packages cream cheese, softened
1 cup sugar
3 eggs
1/2 cup sour cream
3/4 cup Irish cream liqueur

1. In a small bowl stir together crust ingredients. Press firmly onto bottom and halfway up sides of a 9-inch springform pan.
2. In a large bowl using an electric mixer, beat cream cheese until light and fluffy. Gradually beat in sugar. Add eggs, one at a time, beating at low speed until blended. Add sour cream and Irish cream liqueur, beating at low speed until well combined. Pour mixture into crust.
3. Bake in a preheated 300° oven for 50 to 60 minutes. Cheesecake is done when it springs back when lightly touched in the center (cheesecake will shake slightly when moved). Remove the cake from the oven and run a knife around the inside edge of pan.
4. Cool cheesecake on wire rack at room temperature for 1 hour. Cover pan with foil, then chill overnight. Serves 12 to 18.

Kahlúa Chocolate Cheesecake

Crust:
2 cups chocolate cookie crumbs
1/4 cup margarine, melted
Filling:
3 8-ounce packages cream cheese, softened
3/4 cup sugar
3 eggs
3/4 cup sour cream
1 cup milk chocolate chips, melted
1/2 cup Kahlúa
1 teaspoon vanilla extract
Garnish:
Milk chocolate leaves (see page 17)

1. In a small bowl stir together crust ingredients. Press firmly onto bottom and halfway up sides of a 9-inch springform pan.
2. In a large bowl using an electric mixer, beat cream cheese until light and fluffy. Gradually beat in sugar. Add eggs, one at a time, beating at low speed until blended. Add remaining filling ingredients, beating at low speed until well combined. Pour mixture into crust.
3. Bake in a preheated 300° oven for 1 hour to 1 hour and 10 minutes. Cheesecake is done when it springs back when lightly touched in the center (cheesecake is very wobbly when moved). Remove the cake from the oven and run a knife around the inside edge of pan.
4. Cool cheesecake on wire rack at room temperature for 1 hour. Cover pan with foil, then chill overnight.
5. Garnish with milk chocolate leaves. Serves 12 to 18.

Kahlúa Swirl Cheesecake

Crust:
2 cups graham cracker crumbs
1/4 cup sugar
1/4 cup margarine, softened
Filling:
3 8-ounce packages cream cheese, softened
1 cup light brown sugar, packed
3 eggs
3/4 cup sour cream
1/2 cup Kahlúa
2 teaspoons vanilla extract
2 tablespoons milk chocolate chips, melted

1. In a small bowl stir together crust ingredients. Press firmly onto bottom and halfway up sides of a 9-inch springform pan.
2. In a large bowl using an electric mixer, beat cream cheese until light and fluffy. Gradually beat in sugar. Add eggs, one at a time, beating at low speed until blended. Add sour cream, Kahlúa, and vanilla. Beat at low speed until well combined. Transfer 1/3 cup filling to a small bowl. Pour remaining mixture into crust.
3. To reserved 1/3 cup filling, add melted milk chocolate chips. Stir until smooth. Using a spoon drizzle mixture over cheesecake. Cut through mixtures with knife for marble effect.
4. Bake in a preheated 300° oven for 45 to 55 minutes. Cheesecake is done when it springs back when lightly touched in the center (cheesecake will shake slightly when moved). Remove the cake from the oven and run a knife around the inside edge of pan.
5. Cool cheesecake on wire rack at room temperature for 1 hour. Cover pan with foil, then chill overnight. Serves 12 to 18.

Piña Colada Cheesecake

Crust:
1½ cups graham cracker crumbs
1/2 cup flaked coconut
3 tablespoons sugar
3 tablespoons margarine, softened
Filling:
3 8-ounce packages cream cheese, softened
1 cup sugar
3 eggs
1/3 cup sour cream
1/2 cup frozen piña colada concentrate, thawed
2 tablespoons dark rum
2 teaspoons imitation coconut extract
Garnish:
2 cups cubed pineapple
2 tablespoons sugar
2 tablespoons dark rum
Pineapple frond

1. In a small bowl stir together crust ingredients. Press firmly onto bottom and halfway up sides of a 9-inch springform pan.
2. In a large bowl using an electric mixer, beat cream cheese until light and fluffy. Gradually beat in sugar. Add eggs, one at a time, beating at low speed until blended. Add remaining filling ingredients, beating at low speed until well combined. Pour mixture into crust.
3. Bake in a preheated 300° oven for 50 to 60 minutes. Cheesecake is done when it springs back when lightly touched in center (cheesecake will shake slightly when moved). Remove the cake from the oven and run a knife around the inside edge of pan.
4. Cool cheesecake on wire rack at room temperature for 1 hour. Cover pan with foil, then chill overnight.
5. In a medium bowl place 2 cups cubed pineapple. Put sugar and rum into a jar with a lid, then shake to dissolve sugar. Pour liquid over pineapple cubes, tossing to coat thoroughly. Cover, then chill at least 30 minutes or overnight.
6. Remove sides of pan. Place pineapple frond in center of cake. Drain pineapple cubes, discarding liquid. Arrange pineapple cubes around frond. Serves 12 to 18.

Praline Cheesecake

Crust:
2 cups graham cracker crumbs
1/4 cup sugar
1/4 cup margarine, softened
Filling:
3 8-ounce packages cream cheese, softened
1 cup light brown sugar, packed
3 eggs
3/4 cup sour cream
1/2 cup praline-flavored liqueur
2 teaspoons vanilla extract
2/3 cup chopped pecans
1 teaspoon flour
Garnish:
Maple syrup

1. In a small bowl stir together crust ingredients. Press firmly onto bottom and halfway up sides of a 9-inch springform pan.
2. In a large bowl using an electric mixer, beat cream cheese until light and fluffy. Gradually beat in sugar. Add eggs, one at a time, beating at low speed until blended. Add sour cream, praline-flavored liqueur, and vanilla. Beat at low speed until well combined.
3. Pour half the filling into crust. Mix 1/3 cup pecans with 1 teaspoon flour. Sprinkle over filling. Gently spoon remaining filling into pan. Sprinkle with remaining pecans.
4. Bake in a preheated 300° oven for 50 to 60 minutes. Cheesecake is done when it springs back when lightly touched in the center (cheesecake will shake slightly when moved). Remove the cake from the oven and run a knife around the inside edge of pan.
5. Cool cheesecake on wire rack at room temperature for 1 hour. Cover pan with foil, then chill overnight.
6. Garnish individual slices with a drizzle of maple syrup. Serves 12 to 18.

Chocolate Irish Cream Cheesecake

Crust:
2 cups chocolate cookie crumbs
1/4 cup margarine, melted
Filling:
3 8-ounce packages cream cheese, softened
1 cup sugar
3 eggs
1/2 cup sour cream
3/4 cup Irish cream liqueur
4 teaspoons sifted unsweetened cocoa powder
1 cup miniature semisweet chocolate chips
1 teaspoon flour

1. In a small bowl stir together crust ingredients. Press firmly onto bottom and halfway up sides of a 9-inch springform pan.
2. In a large bowl using an electric mixer, beat cream cheese until light and fluffy. Gradually beat in sugar. Add eggs, one at a time, beating at low speed until blended. Add sour cream, Irish cream liqueur, and cocoa. Beat at low speed until well combined.
3. Pour half the filling into crust. Mix 1/2 cup miniature semisweet chocolate chips with 1 teaspoon flour. Sprinkle over filling. Gently spoon remaining filling into pan. Sprinkle remaining miniature semisweet chocolate chips into pan.
4. Bake in a preheated 300° oven for 50 to 60 minutes. Cheesecake is done when it springs back when lightly touched in the center (cheesecake will shake slightly when moved). Remove the cake from the oven and run a knife around the inside edge of pan.
5. Cool cheesecake on wire rack at room temperature for 1 hour. Cover pan with foil, then chill overnight. Serves 12 to 18.

★★★★★★★★★★★★★★★★★★★★★★★★

White Crème de Cacao Cheesecake

Crust:
1¼ cups graham cracker crumbs
2 tablespoons sugar
3 tablespoons margarine, softened
Filling:
3 8-ounce packages cream cheese, softened
1¼ cups sugar
3 eggs
3/4 cup sour cream
1/2 cup white crème de cacao
2 teaspoons vanilla extract
Glaze:
4 ounces white chocolate
2 tablespoons butter
1 tablespoon milk
1 tablespoon white crème de cacao
Garnish:
8 to 10 white chocolate leaves (see page 17)

1. In a small bowl stir together crust ingredients. Press firmly onto bottom of
a 9-inch springform pan.
2. In a large bowl using an electric mixer, beat cream cheese until light and
fluffy. Gradually beat in sugar. Add eggs, one at a time, beating at low speed
until blended. Add remaining filling ingredients, beating at low speed until
well combined. Pour mixture into crust.
3. Bake in a preheated 300° oven for 1 hour to 1 hour and 10 minutes. Cheesecake
is done when it springs back when lightly touched in the center (cheesecake will
shake slightly when moved). Remove the cake from the oven and run a knife around
the inside edge of pan.
4. Cool cheesecake on wire rack at room temperature for 1 hour. Cover pan with
foil, then chill overnight.
5. Place white chocolate, butter, and milk in a small microwave-safe bowl.
Microwave on low power until melted. Stop and stir until smooth. Stir in white
crème de cacao. Cool for 10 minutes. Spread over top of cheesecake. Chill until
glaze is set, about 45 minutes. Garnish edge of cheesecake with white chocolate
leaves. Serves 12 to 18.

Index

★★★

**BUTTERFLY
B O O K S**

4210 Misty Glade
San Antonio, Texas 78247

ORDER FORM

Please send the following books:

Quantity	Title		Total
_____	America's Best Cheesecakes @$12.95	$	_____
_____	Happy Camper's Gourmet Cookbook @$11.95	$	_____

Total for books $_____

Postage and Handling   + $ 2.50

Texas residents add 7 3/4%
sales tax ($1.00 for America's
Best Cheesecakes and $.93 for
Happy Camper's Gourmet Cookbook) $_____

                                                Total $_____

Please make check payable to BUTTERFLY BOOKS.

Mail book(s) to:

Name:_____

Address:_____

City/State/Zip Code:_____

Thank you for your order!